Brand Your Name: Do you know who you are online?

Donna Kakonge

@ Donna Kay Cindy Kakonge

Publisher: Donna Kay Kakonge, MA, ABD

ISBN 978-1-387-11581-5

Brand Your Name: Do you know who you are online?

Brand Your Name: Do you know who you are online?

Introduction

"Life isn't about finding yourself.
Life is about creating yourself."
— George Bernard Shaw

This is a book about branding. Most people understanding branding by what they wear. If they wear something that is from Dolce & Gabbana, then they will be considered to be wearing a high brand. People will also walk around with bags from Harrods's in London just to give themselves the image of wealth that is associated with that store. Branding is a part of our culture and everyone does it.

The type of branding which this book is discussing concerns a more modern form of branding, however, yes, it is about you and how you project your image onto the world. It involves the Internet and the personal image and/or personal reputation that you have online, also known as online personal branding.

Personal branding is an idea that is the brainchild of Tom Peters (1997) [1]. Peter's (1997) article "The Brand Called You," is a vital The concept of personal branding, first popularized by Tom Peters (1997) in his article document in the Age of the Internet when discussing your personal brand.

With the advent of social media, apps, websites, blogs, YouTube.com, Google, Twitter, Instagram, and yes, of course, Facebook, having an online presence, branding your name is a crucial part of your social, business and also sometimes even your private identity. There are more than one billion names which are searched through Google on a daily basis. Google even now has a feature where you can keep track of how many times that your name has been mentioned online. Whether you believe it or not – your name has most likely been searched through Google at least once in your existing lifetime.

Your image, or personal brand, is already on the Internet even if you do not know how to turn on a computer. Here is something to do for fun. Take a moment while you are reading this and just open your web browser. Enter your name into Google. See!!!!!? I bet you found your name. It is this information that the entire world with an Internet connection has access to. Whether it be the president or prime minister of the country in which you live in wanting to know more about the activities that you are involved in that may concern the country. It could be a journalist trying to discover if they should contact you as a source for a story that they are working on. It could be an employer or human resources manager trying to determine if your public profile fits into their company's framework in order to decide whether or not to invite you for an interview for a job. If you are into calling psychics online, it could be a psychic trying to gather information about you in order to make their powers seem real. It could be a friend or family member. Whoever it is – people are constantly searching for other people online, and why? Also, to find out what and how their names are branded and how to do it better.

If you own a business, then here are some things to consider when it comes to owning a personal business and online personal branding.

Meanwell (2003) notes a list of questions to ask yourself before starting out with your own business. If you answer "no" to some of these questions, it may not mean that you are not ready to start your own business – it could be an indication of how successful you will be initially. However, circumstances have a way of changing and as some of the "no" answers turn into "yes" answers, you may start to see your profits soar.

- Are you willing to dedicate long hours for low wages?
- Are you healthy?
- Is your family supportive?
- Have you ever been self-employed?
- Have you worked as a full-time writer before?
- Are you disciplined with money?
- Are you disciplined with time?
- Are you self-motivated?
- Are you good with people?
- Are you a good leader?
- Are you responsible?
- Are you a good decision-maker?

These are some things to keep in mind with owning your own communications or writing business. They are also key points in there that are good to note for working with a production team.

You need to have a business plan:

One of the first things you want to do before you start your own business is writing a business plan. This is basically like your own manifesto for your business.

At the same time, you also need to discover a name for your business. I once read in one of the *Freelancing for Dummies* books that it was good to name your business in your own name. That's what I do. However, if you have a snazzy title for your business and get it registered or incorporated where you live – you're off to a good start. Some people do not officially register their business and do quite well. The choice is yours.

In your business plan you want to include the following information:

- What field will you serve?
- Who is your competition?
- What advantages do you have over the competition? For example, the all-important question to this aspect is why should a company hire you?
- Can you deliver a better product, service, or solution?
- What are your skills and experience, and how can they benefit the business?
- What is the best legal structure for the business?
- How should you keep your business records?
- What insurance do you need? This could be important because you may need to buy into a health insurance package that could protect you if for some reason you can't work
- How will you attract business?
- How will you operate? This includes how will you structure your day?
- Do you need a financial strategy?
- What equipment will you need?
- What will you name your business?
- What space do you need to run a business?

These are all things to keep in mind when you're starting your business. Here are some wise words from Meanwell:

Getting Organized

Quality professionals get it right the first time, every time. The secret of their success relates to systems: a set of procedures developed to ensure that every aspect of their business is coordinated professional and efficiently.

This is true if you work as part of a successful production team too.

Here are some tips from Meanwell (2003) on how to organize your files and information while writing and keeping your business running smoothly:

- Coding files for easy recall: this includes systems such as "PER" for personal files and "HSE" for house files
- Managing information on your desk and computer: suggestions include setting up a separate folder for each client – this is something I do as well

- Dealing with snail mail and email: Meanwell suggests getting that done at the end of the day. Since some of my business is online, I check more frequently
- Backing up data: make sure you keep all your important files on disks or discs to guard against not being to access them from your hard drive
- Handling office supplies and repairs: keep a list of suppliers and "fix-it" people at your fingertips.

Six Easy Habits for Improving Efficiency from Meanwell (2003):

- Keep it clean
- Plan each task each day
- Keep a shopping list
- Get into a routine
- Do tasks in batches
- When you're hot, don't stop.

Meanwell also goes into some tips about working from home. There are some things I can suggest as well.

If you have a huge household to manage or share duties with others, consider renting office space. This can be an extremely efficient way to deal with your time and separate your home life from your work life.

There are many office buildings where you can use their fax machines, bring a laptop or they have computers, get all the services of a receptionist, etc. for low prices.

If you have space and the comfort to work from home – try to section off a convenient place for work. In this case, the kitchen table won't do. It truly helps to have your own room or area just for work.

You can keep whatever policy you like for your office space – personnel only, or allow the occasional person to enter – whatever you like – you're the boss. You may find working styles you've experienced in the past will encourage you to adopt those habits at home if they worked well for you.

There are times where you may want to keep your answering machine on during off hours. While you're working, you may want to make every effort to answer on the first one or two rings.

The style of your writing life must suit your needs as well as your clients. In the book *The New New Journalism* (2007), there are stories about writers whom get up first thing in the morning and write in the mornings, go take a break, then get back to it for the afternoon. There are other stories about people who only write at night. Julia Cameron's

The Right to Write suggests writing in the mornings and calls this practice "morning pages."

We suggest whatever style suits you best is what you need to go with. Finding time to write, especially if you haven't quit your day job yet, can be difficult. There are many stories about people who will even sneak some time to write while they are working.

What is Personal Branding?

"Personal branding entails capturing and promoting an individual's strengths and uniqueness to a target audience," (Labrecque, Markos, & Milne, 2011).

Not everyone may understand exactly what is personal branding right away and/or see a need for it in their life. However, this book will show that everyone needs to have an online profile that is automatically associated with their online personal brand. If you do not control it, other people will. Personal Branding is linked with promoting yourself in positive ways. We will discuss some elements of marketing.

Here is more about online personal branding and aspects it involves.

Imagine you're going to set up your own media business and that online personal branding will help you. Answer the following questions that would go into your business plan:

- What field will you cater to?
- Who is your competition?
- What advantages do you have over the competition? For example, the all-important question to this aspect is why should a company hire you?
- Can you deliver a better product, service, or solution?
- What are your skills and experience, and how can they benefit the business?
- What is the best legal structure for the business?
- How should you keep your business records?
- What insurance do you need? This could be important because you may need to buy into a health insurance package that could protect you if for some reason you can't work
- How will you attract business?
- How will you operate? This includes how will you structure your day?
- Do you need a financial strategy?
- What equipment will you need?
- What will you name your business?
- What space do you need to run a business?

The Advantages of Getting Published

Online personal branding is a lot like publishing online. The next part of this chapter section is on getting published. This is the important part. Like I said before, your brilliant work will do no one any good by sitting in a shoebox under your bed. You have to help your work see the light, even if you write at night. There are many ways to do this.

I've already mentioned many books and articles like Michael Meanwell's *The Wealthy Writer* (2003) that has great suggestions on getting published. As many of you are starting out, some of the things you may want to try are some tips I'll mention here. We'll get back to Meanwell's book later:

- Scour your neighbourhood for free publications that may pay writers to deliver content
- Go on the web and check out e-zines and web sites that may need content
- Develop your own website and publish your material there – any time you publish something to the web that is an act of publishing.
- Check out your local newspapers and community newspapers to find out if you can write for them
- Buy writers guides and writers magazines with a list of places where you can publish

These are just some suggestions. You also need to know the market for your story ideas before you start writing. By using writers markets' guides, you can discover which publications and media companies would be interested in your work. Keeping track of this in a file or a report will make your work to find work easier.

Once you've found the markets to pitch your ideas, you need to write a query letter or pitch the idea to them. We've already gone over proposals, query letters or pitches as they are alternatively called in this class.

Another way of increasing your cache as a writer is to publish an e-book. Michael Meanwell's book *The Wealthy Writer* (2003) first started as an e-book called *The Enterprising Writer*. It later turned into a traditional book.

Here are some words from Meanwell on how to become an E-Publisher:

There are a couple of reasons why you should establish your own Web site.

First, you retain the maximum percentage of profits. Once you've set up your site, you will only need to pay for your ongoing Web hosting and domain fees as well as charges for accepting payments via credit cards. Depending on which providers you select, these costs may represent five to ten percent of the cost of each sale.

Second, by establishing your own site, you have the opportunity to not only promote and sell your books but also showcase your other literary works and skills, and attract more business.

While the rewards can be high, you will need to make a serious investment in understanding how Web marketing works and how to attract and convert visitors to customers – all before you see a serious financial return. If you decide to build your own site, there are many online tools that can help you as well as some good, low-cost, easy-to-use Web development packages.

As stated earlier, the key to Web site success, particularly in our profession, is to keep it simple. The added advantage in doing this is that you do not need to buy expensive Web development programs or hire a Web designer. Your priority should be to design simple Web pages, build credibility with quality products, stimulate interest with convincing copy, and have the ability to safely accept credit card payments and allow e-book downloads from your site. There's a significant investment to be made before you have a successful e-publishing venture, but I assure you that the long-term rewards far outweigh the initial investment.

If you decide to sell your book through another company's website – you can use: www.2checkout.com to sell it. They are a great site that takes only a small commission on sales, allow downloadable products and from a technology and security standpoint work great with e-books. It's also pretty easy to set up for people without much e-commerce experience. Here are some websites to get you started on your way to getting published:

www.getafreelancer.com: this website gives you the chance to register and bid for projects so you can get published with everything from copywriting to e-books. Keep in mind the lowest bid usually gets the project.

www.freelanceworkexchange.com: this another site where you need to register and bid for projects. I wouldn't recommend this one as highly.

canadacareerarts@gmail.com: you may want to check out Don Joyce's Toronto Tonight Magazine.

jobs@swaggnews.com: you may be interested in hip-hop music and this magazine is looking for writers.

www.craigslist.org: this is a great website for looking for writing and even television, radio and film projects.

www.associatedcontent.com: this website is powered by Google and allows you to become a Content Producer building your own website with articles – it's even possible you can make money if you generate enough traffic to your site.

www.myspace.com: this is a place where you can look for jobs and create your own space on the Internet in a community of friends.

www.youtube.com: just bought out by Google, YouTube is huge and you can turn the scripts you've handed into me for class into reality by posting on this site.

www.blogsource.com: this free site based in California allows you to run your own blog and to publish as often as your time allows.

Having a good idea is one of the most important starts to writing. Research is one of the most important parts of writing a good story. The word also means many things in journalism:

- Keeping track of ideas and finding them
- Library Research and Internet Research
- Gathering Research
- Finding Sources

Now, let's discuss some of the story ideas and concepts that will help you to come up with a great online personal brand.

Story Ideas

You are the type of people that are already brimming with many ideas and that helps in this course. Perhaps there's one burning idea you've been waiting to develop and you will get a chance with the backgrounder assignment with this class. You must have ideas to write. Even keeping a shopping list is an idea and when working in journalism, can turn into an extremely interesting topic. Ideas are an extremely important thing. Many working environments where writing is needed also must have a diverse group of people so the ideas become diverse. The exception to this is if it's a community newspaper pertaining to one group of people – or a magazine focused on single mothers. In the latter case, it may help to have many single mothers working at the magazine or on the editorial board. Whatever the publication or opportunity to get your non-fiction published, creating ideas is essential. When a friend and I were discussing how people find ideas, we mentioned how important it is to draw from every aspect of your everyday life. People (and writers especially) are inspired by everything happening around them. Well, perhaps not everything – but, if something peaks your interest – go for it! In the professional writing world, some publications and news agencies pay top dollar for people to conduct focus groups and editorial boards just to diversify their contacts and create story ideas.

You can hold your own focus groups among friends if you feel stumped for ideas. This can be formal or informal. You can throw an "idea party" where everyone there must come with one idea they haven't seen covered often, if at all in writing. While you're sitting around with friends and family, pay attention to the things they say, the things they're concerned about. Being a good listener will make it easier to be a good creative non-fiction writer. There are so many ideas you can come up with just by listening to others.

As well, don't forget that many journalists get their ideas by paying attention to radio, TV, movies, the Internet, books, video games, newspapers and magazines to name a few. The media can inspire you to produce more media.

Here are some solicited words of advice for keeping track of ideas:

- Keep a small notebook to write down ideas
- When you have an idea, write it down if you think it's important
- Depending on how comfortable you feel, share your ideas with others – even if someone else steals it, they won't write it exactly like you would unless they've plagiarized (we'll get into ethics later)
- With the before-mentioned, remember there are some ideas that are so fresh and new – you should keep them to yourself and only share them with people you trust

Keep in mind the ideas you will be sharing with me in this course are yours – not mine. It would be unethical of me to steal any of your stories. This would simply make me look bad. I have a business and don't want that.

We'll get into ethics more lately but many people in the publishing industry are honest contrary to popular belief. Yes, there are always a few bad apples in the bunch. However, because being a successful writer of any genre, including non-fiction is based so much on reputation and spending a lifetime building one – in general, people don't stab others in the back. Keep this in mind and keep paranoia down.

Wow.... that was a lot to say about story ideas. The crazy thing is there's more to say too. This subject could last for days, but let's move onto library research. As well, that's another thing to mention about how to get ideas – sometimes just browsing around a library can create loads of ideas – it's called serendipity.

Library and Internet Research

Libraries and librarians can be your best friends as a non-fiction writer. It's good to develop the skills of library research yourself, but librarians can really help when you're stuck. As well as being trained and educated professionals, they're also usually great at customer service. They love books and media as much as you do. That's how they make their living.

What I'm trying to do here is to also make reference to books that you might be able to find in your local library or on the Internet. I highly encourage you to read all books and Internet references mentioned, as well as to refer to the bibliography that will be included in the addendum.

Also, libraries are the places where you can find the huge dictionaries you may not be able to afford or the *Farmer's Almanac* which you can now find online to create story ideas on upcoming events like anniversaries.

In most libraries around the world, there are also computers where you can use the Internet. Most of these computers, such as the ones in Canadian libraries, allow you to access the local and national databases of resources. Also, there are links to resources where you can access other resources all over the world and suggestions for finding ideas:

- www.nytimes.com/learning - offers an "On This Day in History" archive that is great for doing stories on anniversaries.
- There's also *The Optimist's Guide to History* and *Pro Football Chronicle* that give you information on important dates in history for stories
- To get out of a writing rut, try reading things you don't usually read, like *Aeronautics Monthly* or *Modern Ferret*
- Shake up your life to come up with interesting stories
- Take a vacation or a break
- When finding sources, good places to start – ProfNet (www.profnet.com), sponsored by PR Newswire
- Again, when finding sources, ExpertSource (www.businesswire.com), backed by Business Wire
- Ask other writers – you can connect to other writers through MySpace.com or Facebook.com, the American Society of Journalists and Authors, the Periodical Writers Association of Canada and the Writer's Guild of Canada, etc.

- Use professionals for expert advice, there is an *Encyclopaedia of Associations* at your local library
- Public Relations people or PR people can be your friends for stories. Places like the University of Southern California have databases of experts: (http://uscnews.usc.edu/experts/index.html)
- Guest finder (www.guestfinder.com) can put you in the direction of people who are experts
- Go through your own contacts

Simple ways of doing research include using popular search engines like Google.com and Yahoo.com. These search engines will give you access to many books.

The Internet itself has many resources that can be helpful. However, keep in mind just like with books – you must use the information with caution. It is sometimes said few people are more cynical than writers – this is not true for all; however, if you possess this quality, use it to your advantage. There are many ways to check if the information you receive is valid. Always get at least a second opinion if you can, unless you're sure the first opinion is accurate. Go with your heart, gut, and head when finding information – your credibility as a journalist counts on it.

Gathering Research

Gathering information is a difficult task and sometimes becomes a burden. For some writers, this is the best part of writing, for others – they can't stand it. I recommend reading *The New New Journalism* (Boynton, 2007) book I mentioned before to find out how many writers of non-fiction handle research, but I will go into some points here.

There are stories you will do creatively that will take you anywhere from minutes (depending on how fast you type)…to years. It depends on what your interests are and how complicated the story. Something like a memoir, for example, is something you may do when you're forty years old and still writing, expecting to publish in another forty years. Patience is an important thing to have with writing.

However, you may be working for a literary magazine where stories are produced month by month. You may also be working for a newspaper's Lifestyles section where stories are produced on a daily basis. You may also have your own website with advertising and earn a comfortable living and writing all day long as many stories as you can churn. As you can see, the situations vary.

Tom Wolfe, a pioneer in creative non-fiction, also known as the New Journalism, once said that you practically have to sleep with your subjects to really get to know them.

Literally, this need not be true, however, this does raise an important point that Dan Wakefield mentions in his 1966 book called *Between the Lines* about the new journalism:

> I am writing now for those readers – including myself – who have grown increasingly mistrustful of and bored with anonymous reports about the world, whether signed or unsigned, for those who have begun to suspect what we reporters of current events and problems so often try to conceal: that we are really individuals after all, not all-knowing, all-seeing Eyes but separate, complex, limited, particular "I"s.

With traditional online personal branding, many times a reader can sense the complete detachment involved in the reporting. Why so many readers love non-fiction and why so many writers love doing it is because it creates connections in this world where six degrees of separation means a lot. The more we know about a person, the better we can connect to them and the message they're trying to get across.

So, you don't need to get into bed with your sources, but you do need to understand them…. to just about get to the point where you can read their minds.

Finding Sources

Your research should help you to find sources. Through Internet searches, looking for people in the library, the person you talk to at the hot dog stand, your dentist, the sales associate you bought your shoes from – all these people are potential sources.

With the style of story for your writing, such as a memoir or personal piece, you may not have to go far or search wide for your sources.

We all have contacts – some of us may have the Queen of England on our list, some of us may have the butcher's name down the street. Depending on the story, all contacts are equally important. I recommend using a spreadsheet or finding special database software to keep your contacts handy.

Make sure as you keep this list, you also keep notes about this person so you can remember them. Keep in mind this contact list could become public so use discretion when taking your notes about someone.

Finding sources is also about networking. Networking, or also simply put, getting to know as many people as you can, is important as a writer. Although writing can be a solitary service, you still need to take some time out of your schedule getting to know people.

Audience Analysis

Advertisers seek audiences who are most likely to buy their products or services. A product designed for women between seventeen and thirty-nine – cosmetics, for example – would not be advertised on a program that reaches a predominantly male audience, such as sports who. Once the target audience is determined, the commercial is designed to appeal to the specific needs and want of that audience. Audience analysis is called demographics, which may include such information as age, gender, economic level, political orientation, occupation, educational level, ethnic background, geographical concentration, and product knowledge. Psychographics, even more, detailed audience analysis, includes such elements as a lifestyle, primary interests, and attitudes and beliefs.

Although writers attempt to appeal to the largest number of people expected to watch the program and the commercial, you must take care not to spread the message too thin. Television audiences tuned to network programs tend to be dis-unified demographically. Independent local or regional stations can determine audience demographics more easily because of the smaller number of viewers limited to a smaller area. Local cable systems can determine demographics most accurately, serving a prescribed area and knowing exactly who their subscribers are. Most radio stations have highly structured formats, appealing to specific audiences in their communities, so each station can determine its demographics with relative ease.

After analyzing as fully as possible the audience likely to view the commercial, the writer consciously includes materials that appeal to that audience. The same audience analysis criteria apply to public service announcements.

Audience analysis is then combined with specific needs and wants appeals within the commercial to make the most effective impact. Before this step, however, the writer must be thoroughly familiar with the product or service to be advertised.

Familiarization with the Product – You and Your Business

In addition to personal observation or use of the product, the writer should collect as much information about it as possible from those connected with it. A good source of information is the research or promotion department of the advertiser's company. Develop receptive and flexible attitudes toward products and services. Aside from ethical considerations, you may be given the assignment for a product or service that seems totally dull and uninteresting to you. In fact, it may seem the same way to the majority of the potential customers. Your job is to make it exciting.

If you are given a new instant camera to promote that is easy to load, has a self-focusing, long-distance lens, uses fast colour film, can be carried in your pocket, and costs half as much as the comparable competitive models, your job as a copywriter is relatively easy. The writers who first developed the commercials in the United States for a low-cost, high-gas-mileage, long-lasting-engine small car with large seating capacity and storage space made Volkswagen at one time the largest selling foreign automobile in the U.S.

On the other hand, you may have to deal with a seemingly boring product like a pill for indigestion, or the services of one of the many clone-like fast food chains, or a long-standing and accepted product like telephone service. Creative copywriters greatly increased the sales of all three of these advertisers by developing unique and novel ways of presenting their wares, and coming up with ads that had the entire country saying, "Try it, you'll like it," "Take a break today," and "Reach out and touch someone."

Appeals

The third important factor in preparing a commercial or online personal branding is to appeal to the audience's basic needs or wants. All viewers and listeners are motivated by essential psychological and intellectual concerns, some conscious, and most subconscious. By playing on these motivations, the copywriter can make almost anything and, in many cases, even persuade the audience to take some action – such as running right out and buying the product or phoning a nine-hundred-number to purchase a service.

Three basic appeals, applied through the ages and based on Aristotle's three key elements of persuasion – ethos, logos, and pathos – translate today as ethical, logical, and emotional appeals.

Ethical Appeal

Aristotle called persuasion by someone recognized as a "good person" an ethical appeal. When a well-known or well-respected person tells us something, we tend to believe it more than if the same statement had come from a non-celebrity. For example, we not only buy products advertised by entertainment stars, but we even pay attention to political and social comments by a pop singer or a hockey player, whose actual knowledge of the subject may be nil. Later we'll discuss the testimonial as one principal commercial form. The testimonial is based on ethical appeal.

A further application of ethos or ethical appeal relates the concept of the product or the manner in which the product is present to the audience's ethical values. Of course, this varies in different sections of the world and even within the same market and is determined by psychographics surveys.

Logical Appeal

The logical appeal is exactly what it says. The persuasion is based on the facts, attempting to convince the potential buyer that the product or service fills a logical, practical need. For example, study the next commercial you see for an automobile. Does it recommend that you buy the car because its shorter length will make it easier for the owner to find a parking space in most cities? Because the cars lower horsepower will save on gasoline? Because it's fewer cylinders limit its speed and might not only prevent speeding tickets but also perhaps save its passengers' lives as well? If so, then the ad appeals to logic. Note, however, what most car ads really do appeal to – under emotion appeals?

How many ads can you remember that have consisted principally of logical appeals?

There aren't many. Ads for most space-age electronics, such as compact disc players, camcorders, and stereo systems usually emphasize styling, size, and decibel count rather than quality, construction, and durability. Some commercials, however, do use logical appeals. Computer hardware and software ads frequently stress the computer's greater capacity and flexibility and the software's multiple uses, although many of the prospective customers don't need the complexity of the product they are being motivated to buy or are not aware that the rapid advances and changes in the computer field may make their expensive new purchase obsolete within months or even weeks.

Many commercials only appear to use logical appeals. Closer examination reveals the appeals are really emotional in content, the most used and most effective type of advertising.

Emotional Appeals

An emotional appeal does not mean one that evokes laughter or tears, but one that appeals to the non-logical, non-intellectual aspects of the viewer's or listener's personality. It is an appeal to the audience's basic needs or wants. Take the automobile advertising example. Most car ads emphasize size, power, and styling. Even compact cars are sold with the slogan "big car room." Television ads show cars driving at powerful ultra-high speeds, zooming dangerously around curves on small country roads. Some automobile commercials stress the logic of family use, even though emphasizing the size to accommodate many people and the power to carry them. Most auto ads highlight design and equipment by featuring passengers who look like movie stars, with the implication that people who drive these automobiles associate with beautiful, rich people or that if you own that car you will certainly attract them.

These are emotional appeals: appeals to feelings rather than reason. These auto commercial approaches appeal to basic emotional needs: power, prestige, and good taste. The power to attract love or sex partners, the power to move quickly without any impediment through life, the prestige of associating with prestigious people, the prestige of owning something that draws envy from others, the good taste to more than keeping up with the Joneses.

Other emotional appeals that have proven highly motivating in commercials and PSAs are the love of family, as evidenced in insurance company commercials, patriotism, good taste reputation, religion, and loyalty to a group. Conformity to public opinion is effectively used in advertisements for young people's clothes that may be torn, discoloured, and even uncomfortable, but promoted as necessary for peer acceptance. The appeal to self-preservation is perhaps the strongest emotional appeal of all. Drug commercials, among others, make good use of this technique.

Organization of Commercial or Announcement for Online Personal Branding

The purpose of the commercial or announcement is to persuade. Many experts in rhetoric have developed systems for persuasion. College students usually are exposed to such systems in elementary communication, business, or philosophy courses. Essentially, five steps of persuasion can be applied to virtually every television or radio commercial or online personal branding:

- Get the audience's attention.
- After you get the audience's attention, hold its interest.
- Create an impression that some sort of problem exists, related to the function of the product or service being presented.
- Plant the idea that using the particular product or service can solve the problem.
- Finish with a strong emotional and/or logical and/or ethical appeal to motivate the audience to take action on the product or service: put it on a grocery list, mail in a donation to a charity, or run right out and buy whatever it is.

In most cases the immediate action is, of course, not obtained, and the audience may not consciously make a written or mental note to do anything about it. But all of another, or us, at one time, have bought or done something that we likely would not have, had we not been influenced, even subconsciously, by the television or radio announcements for that product or service.

Formats

The five major format types for commercials and PSAs are the straight sell, the testimonial, humour, music, and the dramatization. Any single announcement can combine two or more of these approaches:

- The Straight Sell: This should be a clear, simple statement about the product or service. Don't involve the announcer or station too closely with what is being sold or promoted, except, of course, when the announcement is a promo for the station itself or a fund-raising or other support spot for a cause or organization with which the station and its personnel want to be publicly associated. The writing should stress something special about the product or service, real or implied. Sometimes the straight sell is built around a slogan characterizing that special attribute. Straight sell approach can result in an announcement that not only is effective in promoting the product or service but also captures the public's imagination and interest.

- The Testimonial: For the celebrity testimonial to be effective, its content and style, including the setting, action, and type of dialogue, must be consistent with the public image of the personality. The audience must believe that the celebrity really believes what he or she is saying about the product or service. Promotion of a product, such as a toy or cereal, by someone admired by youngsters – for instance, the host of the television program on which the commercial is featured – may have an undue and unfair influence. Children are easily susceptible to such promotion. Testimonial from the average man or woman – the worker, the homemaker, the person in the street with whom the viewer or listener at home can directly identify is an alternative to the celebrity. Through such identification, the viewer may more easily accept the existence of the common problem in a commonly experienced physical, economic, or vocational setting and consequently, more readily accept the solution adopted by the person in the commercial.

- Humour: Humour is always an effective attention-getter, but successful humour must reflect current humorous trends. The gag or one-liner was once the staple of advertising humour, but has now been largely replaced by satire and parody. Most humour is used in conjunction with dramatization, tied to a story line or to character relationships. Some humour is bizarre, but if part of a continuingly interesting gimmick, as in the Parkay commercial, it can be highly successful. Other humour can be gentle, almost with a tinge of pathos. And some humour is effective because of its incongruity or an unanticipated switch in thought.

- Music: The musical commercial has always been one of the most effective methods for predisposing an audience to remember a product. How many times have you listened to a song on radio or television, been caught up in its cadence, and then suddenly realized it was a commercial and not the latest hit tune?

Special Considerations

Although most commercial writers are aware of ethical considerations, such as role stereotyping, many are not sensitive to the special characteristics of many segments of the population that determine those audiences' reactions to specific commercial stimuli.

Audience analysis must go beyond the perception that all viewers or listeners of the same age, gender, economic, education, and geographical demographics, for example, will react the same way.

Dr. Cecil Hale, a communications professor and former president of the National Association of Television and Radio Artists, believes there must be a common understanding, a mutual feeling among the writer, announcer, and audience for any broadcast material, including advertising spots, to be optimally effective. Hale thinks that the writer must find relationships among the character of the product, the character of the audience, and the character of the occasion. Commercials for the same product need to be different for different audiences because the audiences see the product differently. Not all people in a given ethnic or racial group are alike. Hale warns against stereotyping any segment of the audience. Two African-American oriented or Latino-oriented stations in the same community may deal with different audiences, just as would two white-oriented stations.

Caroline Jones, as creative director of the Black Creative Group, advising ad agencies dealing with the Black market, remarked in Joel Dreyfuss's *Washington Post* article, "Blacks and Television," that "they are getting blacks in ads, but they are not doing black ads. It's not a black lifestyle." Referring to studies showing that Black women in general cook foods longer than do white women, and add more spices, stressing taste rather than speed, Jones said that a Black-oriented commercial, "instead of saying, "You can cook it in a minute," should say 'You will have more to spend with your family.' I'm talking about why they use a product, why they buy it. They haven't researched it."

The same principles apply to all audiences, and the writer who analyzes the audience's distinct varying attitudes, backgrounds, and lifestyles will more accurately find the common ground between product and audience.

Here are some assignment suggestions:

- Choose a product, a television program, and a television station. Write a 30-second commercial script and storyboard for the product. Justify what you've prepared by stating (1) your audience analysis, (2) emotional and/or logical and/or ethical appeals, and (3) steps of persuasion used.
- Write the same commercial project for radio, considering the differences between the two media.
- Using the same considerations, prepare an online personal branding for television and for radio.

- Write an ID for a television and a radio station.
- Write a promo for a television and a radio station.

Examples of corporate media programming include "talk" programs that feature managers or subject area experts discussing new sales approaches, manufacturing processes, or organizational changes, among other topics; teleconferencing, small or large meetings connecting to or more sites via television; executives giving speeches to employees or to the public at large; company leadership being interviewed for internal or external distribution; and formal education and training programs.

Feature and documentary formats provide historical, scientific, public service, operational, or another background regarding the company that will enhance its institutional image. News formats convey information about the company on a periodic, sometimes daily basis.

All companies use commercials and announcements. News, features, and commercials have been merged into a format that has grown in recent years, sometimes called "infomercials." These range from short commercial spots, usually about 30 seconds that combine public service information, such as consumer data with a commercial message, to fifteen and thirty-minute and longer programs that sell a product or service.

The feature/documentary and commercial have been united for public relations programs. For example, if the company wanted to expand onto some property that was going to be used for low-income housing, a feature-type commercial showing how the company's expansion will provide jobs for low-income families, below-market-rate loans for worker home-ownership and another suitable site for housing could defuse opposition to expansion and gain increased support for the company and its products.

Perhaps the most widely served corporate purpose is education and training. Many companies produce video training programs internally. Some have highly sophisticated production centres and a staff of producers and writers (usually, the producer and writer are the same people – an important consideration for students who are studying production but neglecting writing courses). Training videos are produced for all corporate levels and for all purposes. Programs run the gamut from introducing the physical surrounding in which new employees will work to more sophisticated requirements such as filing procedures for entry-level office personnel, to more complex procedures such as operating a given mass production machine, to an even higher level such as introducing the development of a new company product based on a recently invented scientific process.

Although writing any format is essentially the same for all media distribution situations, remember that corporate media's bottom line may not relate directly to selling the product. The company's purpose with any given video, slide show, or audiotape can vary greatly: to enhance employee morale, obtain good public relations, sell, persuade colleagues, or educate and train. The writer must determine the company's specific purpose for any given corporate media program.

Corporate media writing is not confined to industry. Though widely used in industry, corporate media refers as well to media use by government offices, educational systems and institutions, and professional and civic associations and organizations – in other words, by any group that wants to inform, persuade, or educates, internally and externally.

Corporate Programs Procedure

Objectives

To develop an idea for a program, the writer must know the program's purpose. Usually, there are two major objectives: that of the client or management and that of the target audience. It generally is easier to determine the purposes of an in-house production because management usually is precise about what it wants the media program to accomplish.

The writer must determine, as well, the purposes of the audience. If a training program is aimed at company employees, as most corporate media programs are, how is the intended audience going to be motivated to watch and pay attention to the program and to actually learn from it and follow through on the management goals inherent in it?

Demographics are important here for two major reasons. The first and perhaps most obvious, the reason is the same as that for writing commercials: determining what kinds of interest, and persuade them to do whatever it is management wants them to do. The second relates to motivation: determining why the viewer or listener should take the program seriously. Every member of the audience must be made aware of what is in it for him or her.

Will learning the new production technique and using it successfully earn a raise or a promotion?

Is proper use of the new computer system necessary for keeping one's job?

Will expanded sales of the new product result in escalated commissions?

Does learning how to make good speeches, to increase participation as a middle manager in community affairs, result in higher bonuses?

If the production is for public consumption, such as an institutional feature or an infomercial, the writer uses the public demographics of the target community.

A good example of combining management's purpose with motivating the audience both to watch and learn is "The Hantel Advantage" script.

Treatment or Outline

The treatment is important as the next step in maintaining agreement between writer and client/management during the preparation and production period. It might well cost the writer time and money, and perhaps even the job itself, for the client/management to look at a script several weeks after the beginning of the process and object that it is not at all what the client had in mind, wanted, or expected to get. Therefore, soon after the initial meeting the writer should prepare an outline and get client/management approval before beginning a detailed treatment, which in turn needs approval before the preliminary script is written. That, as well, should be approved before the final script is prepared. In other words, the writer should be certain that his or her work is on target during every phase of the project.

There are exceptions. Some in-house and independent writers have worked sufficiently long and successfully for the company that their judgment and proficiency are trusted. These writers may be given the project purpose at an initial meeting and told to come back with a completed script in a specified time period. Experienced writers-producers such as Ralph De Jong, whose script is used as an illustration of good writing later in this lecture are frequently in that position. As you read De Jong's advice to young writers note that despite his prerogatives he takes the steps necessary to be certain that both he and the client agree all the way.

Research

In most cases, research takes the longest time unless the writer happens to be an expert in the subject being scripted. Although the program should be entertaining as well as educational, it is not an entertainment program. Its purpose is to convey specific ideas and information. It must be totally accurate. To make it interesting, the writer must become familiar with all aspects of the subject, whether the company history or the technical operation of a scientific process. Only then can the writer have enough material to choose the options that will result in the most effective script. Depending on the subject, the writer will do library research, computer research on the Internet, pick the brains of experts, and talk with the employees who are the targets of the program and with the management officials who decided on the objectives. Roger Sullivan advised the writer to "work closely with subject matter experts and rely on their comments, as well as on your own imagination."

When possible, the writer seeks real-life experience with the subject, such as going into the field with an insurance salesperson and applying the new method promoted in the program, working on the assembly line with the new machine, or accompanying the vice-presidents who are promoting the company's image at community affairs.

Production

When the final script is prepared and approved, production starts. In the corporate situation, unlike many broadcast or cable circumstances, the writer's job usually does not end with the completed script, but can continue through the editing and screening process. There is always the chance the company president, seeing for the first time a program that has been approved every step of the way by a cadre of vice-presidents, will ask for some changes before the programs are used.

Evaluation

A final step takes place after the program is used: an evaluation. Has the program been effective? Did it accomplish management's purposes? Were the audience's needs satisfied? The writer should participate in measuring the program's effects, usually through traditional educational tools of testing and interview, to know how more effectively to write the next program or series.

Writing Techniques

For educational video, the shadow script is a transcription of the classroom teacher's presentation of a particular subject and a minimum rewriting of the transcription for smoother continuity and subsequent voice-over recording by a professional.

Many corporate scripts, whether for video or film, use the drama format, creating suspense that holds the audience and a conflict whose solution achieves the presentation's objective. Corporate film writer-director Richard Bruner, who effectively used dramatic dialogue and action rather than the voice-over narration and lecture-type dialogue that dominate many corporate videos, offered some advice in an article in *Audio-Visual Communications* by Thomas C. Hunter. Bruner explained that when the purpose of the program is simply conveying expository information, narration can do a good job. But "for a film to have a dramatic impact," he advised a dramatic format. "The audience must be convinced that something important is at stake. The protagonist must have a stake in the outcome of the conflict."

The "talking head" and "straight sell narrative" rarely work well in the corporate training script and are to be avoided in most situations. How then does the writer convey the system, routine, procedure, or ideas that result in effective learning? Corporate training scripts rely on two major approaches: the right way–wrong-way demonstration and the step-by-step demonstration.

In the right way–wrong-way demonstration a character uses the system or machine incorrectly, with unwanted and unhappy consequences. A character doing it the right way follows this. The process can be shown step-by-step if desired, so that every stage is absolutely clear. For example, a restaurant chain may contract for a video that teaches new personnel how to serve wine. In one sequence the novice manages to push the cork into the bottle; put a red wine bottle into an ice bucket; pour the wine without showing the wine label, offering the cork for odour, or providing a preliminary taste; fill each glass to the top; and then, of course spill wine onto the tablecloth and the customer's clothes. Treated with humour, and followed by a demonstration how to serve wine correctly, the sequences who the audience the correct procedure and the common mistakes to avoid.

Humour is an effective device for most script formats; it's risky, however, in the corporate script. Many writers have found that a sense of humour often is not appreciated. Some corporate executives seem to equate humour in the script with making fun or light of their product or service. Further, comedy writing is extremely difficult. Many writers think they are funny, but often they are guilty of sophomoric humour. Corporate producers will tell you that they've rarely seemed humour work in corporate scripts.

A second major approach to effective learning in the training script is a step-by-step demonstration. The expert, office manager, or production unit chief can demonstrate point-by-point how to do the particular task. Slow motion, close-ups, repetition can reinforce the demonstration and key scripted questions from the character or characters playing the learning-employees roles. When the demonstration is completed, the person playing the learner may then be asked to go over the process point-by-point.

Reinforcement and repetition are extremely important. Tell the audience what you are going to tell them, tell them, and then tell them what you've told them. Sum up after each learning module, and sum up at the end of the program. Complex processes should be repeated slowly enough for each aspect to be made clear. Visual action, voice and sound effects, music, written words – usually in large block letters – and diagrams – in colour where possible and always clear and precise – are good supports.

The corporate script is more formal than the entertainment script.

Here are some writing techniques tips:

- Use the active voice instead of the passive whenever possible. Many writers tend to use the words "there is" – the passive voice – rather than stating the facts or ideas directly or actively; for example, "There are twelve steps to this dance" instead of "This dance has twelve steps."

- Use simple, colloquial language, suited to the level of the audience. You are not writing print literature, but visual and aural presentations. Construct the rhythm and pace of the language in the script to the subject matter and temper of the program. Keep sentences short, especially with how-to demonstrations. Don't try to cram too many ideas into a short time period. A principal drawback in most neophyte scripts is the overload of information, making it difficult for the audience to keep up with, much less remember, everything presented.

- Be exact. Be precise. The audience should have no doubt about what is being said or shown, or what it should be learning. Don't assume that all the audience members understand all the technical language just because the audience is an employee group. Explain and define all technical terms. On the other hand, you should determine what specialized words or terms is common knowledge for that audience and, where appropriate, in place of more formal terms that might need more explanation.

- Use the right word and spell it correctly. Just as you should do for all writing in any situation, don't hesitate to use your dictionary and thesaurus. If you work with a computer or word processor, most writing format software includes both a thesaurus and a spelling checker.

- Be direct in training programs. For example, when instructing the audience about how to use a new machine, don't have the demonstrator say, "Next, you should release the thingamabob, and then you should spin it through the Fraga Maran..." simply write: "Next, release the thingamabob and spin it through the fragrant..."

- Think visually, write visually, and revise visually. Most corporate scripts are visual – either filmed or taped video or slides. Many writers have a tendency to think of instructional writing as print writing because most of their experience with such learning is with textbooks.

- Be neat. Neatness counts. Make a good impression with what you submit. If your script looks sloppy, the people deciding whether to hire you may assume that your work, in general, is sloppy. The corporate world has little patience with artistic bohemianism.

Before we get to watch the rest of the videos, I'll give you your assignment and we can discuss it.

Here are your choices:

- Choose a business or industry in your area, it could be your own business and that is large enough to benefit from a media-training program. Discuss with its training, sales, or human resources director some of its current needs and prepare a half-hour video script or proposal designed to solve a specific problem.
- Prepare a fifteen-minute script, either video or audio, that can be used to orient new members of a campus organization of which you are a member.
- Prepare a treatment for the pilot of a half-hour educational documentary series that would air on a local television or radio or cable system.

Online Personal Branding and the Science of Marketing

According to Chron (Linton, 2017), the five stages of the business to business buying process are first awareness. With this step, each business involved with the business to business buying process must be aware of the products, services, and items that each business has for sale (Linton, 2017). Once this is established, then it is possible for the businesses involved to form alliances (Linton, 2017). Once the alliances are formed, also known and understood as awareness, then the business to the business process of buying can take place (Linton, 2017). The next stage of this business to business buying process is specification (Linton, 2017). Within the business contracts among the business to business buying transactions, there need to be clear specifications of the quantity that is desired in the transaction, the price per unit and also the total price of the transaction, as well as any taxes that may apply and/or shipping fees as well plus many other business transactional issues (Linton, 2017). Once the specifics, or specifications are clearly understood, written out and agreed upon by both if not a number of business parties involved then the business to business buying process can begin the steps towards being finalized (Linton, 2017). The next steps of the business to business buying process are proposals (Linton, 2017). Proposals necessary in order to ascertain whether the right business with the exact products, items and or services are available in order to ensure that the business to business buying process can continue (Linton, 2017). Once the proposal is offered from one business to another business and then accepted and/or declined, this also creates either a continuation and/or a brief ending of the business to business transaction process (Linton, 2017). If a proposal is accepted, it would also be highly likely that the businesses involved would continue to do business together (Linton, 2017). However, even if a proposal is rejected, this would not necessarily mean that the businesses could not work with one another in future and at another time in the business to business buying process (Linton, 2017). The next step would be the evaluation (Linton, 2017). In this step of the process, there would need to be a clear evaluation of the outcomes of the business to business buying process – that is would it be something where each business is clearly satisfied with the business transaction and the products, items and services sold and bought (Linton, 2017). The last step in the business to business buying process is "order," (Linton, 2017). This is the final stage of the business to business buying process and once all of the previous stages of the process have been successfully completed then one party and or parties in question (be they business (es) in this case), as well as the seller of the products, items and services would receive the order and the business buying would make the order (Linton, 2017).

This question will identify and describe three common governmental/political activities that significantly influence a firm's ability to sell goods and services in a global marketplace. The three common governmental/political activities that significantly influence a firm's ability to sell goods and services in a global marketplace are trade and tariff regulations with particular countries, trade embargos and political bans on specific countries that are violating human rights laws. With the trade and tariff regulations to particular countries, these trade and tariff regulations are governmental intervention in order to ensure fair trade between America and other countries in terms of goods and services bought and sold. Since the American dollar is so high on the global marketplace, a firm would need to offer fair prices and fair compensation to any global employees that are off-site from America's lands in order to do business with that country through government intervention. At times, the government steps in and ensures that when a country is violating certain global laws that there will be a trade embargo – basically American companies are blocked, banned and prevented from doing any kind of business with a particular country and or particular countries. In a situation such as this, most of the times the reasons for this occurring are based not just on governmental policies, but also on political philosophies and the overall impressions of American people towards the country and/or countries in question in order to prevent the financial growth of another country in which ideologically America does not agree with their conduct. When a country is a human rights violator, America will often not allow companies to do business, sell goods and services, with that country as well. It is similar to a trade embargo, however, is based on human rights grounds. For example, during World War II, America did not do business with Germany because of the Holocaust to Jewish People.

This question will discuss how Marketers can extend a product's life cycle. In an example of a vehicle, a car – the way that the life cycle of any car can be extended would be by continuously encouraging the company to come out with a variety of models of the vehicle that will suit the lifestyle choices of a variety of people. I will take Nissan as an example. Nissan has the Sentra. This latter vehicle is expensive and affordable to people that mainly would have a double income in the home. Nissan also has the Elantra. This vehicle would be possible for a single income person to own, however, the person would need to be a high-income earner. On the other hand, Nissan also markets the Nissan Micra. The Nissan Micra is a new vehicle that just came out about two or three years ago by Nissan. With this vehicle, it is possible to purchase and to own a vehicle for as low as $14,000 which in many cases is even less than what the average American pays in tuition costs per year to go to university. Marketers did a good job by marketing the Nissan Micra to appeal to that average of society that may be in need of a new vehicle, however, cannot afford to purchase an expensive one that is out of their budget.

The reason why it is more difficult for a Marketer to be part of a marketing landscape that is monopolistic, rather than purely competitive is the focus of this answer. In a monopolistic business society, it is money and those who have the most wealth who win. In a purely competitive marketplace, it is those with the best ideas who win. This is why, since the career of Marketing does attract creative people, it would be difficult to put forth even the best ideas without the money to showcase this idea in a CNN commercial spot done by a "boring monopolistic" business as just an example.

Walt Disney characters will no longer promote unhealthy foods. This is wise. This is what is known as a socially responsible bottom line. When a company has a socially responsible bottom line, they understand that you can actually earn money by doing good deeds. A company then understands that good people do win in this world and good efforts are rewarded and the power that these companies have in our society, particularly one such as Walt Disney that has been around for so long, has a responsibility to give back to society and "do the right thing."

The difference between focus group research and test marketing will be the focus of this answer. Focus group research is a collective activity where a group of people gathers and are asked questions in order to determine what their values, concerns, opinions, preferences, dislikes, and likes, as well as their suggestions, are concerning a product, service and or item. Test marketing is when a company decides to put a new Cornflake cereal product out on the market in order to find out if people will buy it. They may call the new Cornflake cereal – Pepsi Cornflake Cereal – and the two companies have joined to create a cornflake that also tastes like Pepsi soda. This product would be put out on the market in order to determine if it is successful or not.

The way that stores can capitalize on the benefits that they receive from customers is to encourage more customers to do surveys, to tell other people about good service or enjoyment of products and items that they received from the store, to offer more contests and prizes to their customers so it will encourage them to keep coming back to the store, plus to offer a loyalty rewards programs. With all of these services and much more, the business will continue to blossom and bloom.

To understand what personal branding online is going beyond just a search of your name in Google, let's clear up some of the terminologies that surrounds personal branding. Personal branding can be classified into three basic kinds of branding. These kinds of branding are as follows: corporate branding, product branding, and personal branding. What we discussed in the latter chapter to give you a sense of how personal branding works is an example of putting your name on a Google search. This is just the first step to understanding personal branding.

Branding, as you would also think about it through products branding such as Nike, Coca-Cola, Pepsi, British Airways, and even the Olympics and/or World Cup Soccer are all elements of a product and/or also associated with events in some cases which have a brand. This product branding is also associated with corporate branding as well. All types of branding, from corporate, to products, to personal, are the kind of perceptions that the public has about the source which is being branded, the kind of image that the source has publicly, and ultimately, the most important aspect of branding is the reputation in which the source which is being branded has on the public at large.

Billions of people on this planet use the Internet and social media in order to make themselves "stand out from the crowd" in this world. They may do it for business and professional reasons in regards to their career; they may do it in order to raise their beauty image online, they may do it for fundraising purposes and raising capital purposes, as well as marketing purposes. Many people also just want to meet other interesting people online and they know by carefully sculpting and crafting their online image, they will meet exactly who they want to meet, rather than who they do not want to meet online – for a variety of purposes, including business and professional reasons.

According to Barnett (2010), "self-branding is about thinking of [an individual] as a brand – a product that can be viewed strategically and creatively in a competitive market to bring maximum value to [the individual] and [their] company."

With personal branding, one can carve out a distinct image of themselves online that will remain permanently there for as long as the Internet to is online. Personal branding is also a great way for individuals to communicate and express themselves, plus their skill set and their attributes to the worldwide marketplace that accesses the Internet.

The definition of personal branding is that it is the system where people and self-employed businesses stand out from the crowd online through the promotion of their unique attributes, skill sets and values on a personal and/or professional level in order to deliver a clear and powerful message to the online public with a desired outcome in mind (Schawbel, 2010, p. 6).

Although we have defined what is online personal branding, there are still many misconceptions concerning exactly what is online personal branding and many people thought that they do not need to be involved with it, nor, that it concerns their lives. The next chapter on misconceptions about personal branding will help to clarify and reinforce the importance of online personal branding for you and other people you know. Not just for business reasons, but for personal reasons as well.

Misconceptions about Personal Branding?

This section of the book will be interesting. It will address many of the misconceptions that many people have about online personal branding. After reading this, you may have many new perspectives concerning previous thoughts that you had held concerning online personal branding.

Although everything that has been said so far about personal branding has been positive, there are some common misunderstandings and misconceptions which surround personal branding. This section of the book will discuss what these misconceptions about personal branding are.

Many people believe that the title of their company, their business, or even their personal titles such as a doctor, constable, your honour, your worship, is all titles which already give a distinct and a unique personal brand to the individual. However, with so many people in this world being granted such distinguished titles in this day and age, these distinguished titles no longer hold the same importance to personally brand someone as they used to even twenty years ago.

Many people also believe that the personal effort and the personal time that it takes in order to create a personal brand online is far too time-consuming and that the time involved could be far better spent. This book would respectfully argue that the Internet is a powerful force and one must prioritise things in their life. It is actually important and should be prioritised to promote your personal brand online. More people are even cutting their cabled television and beginning to turn on to the Internet in order to know what is going on in the world. What do you want the world to know about you? If you do not control your personal brand – someone else will. The sad thing is that you may not like what they have to say.

Others believe that their logo is their brand. However, there are so many logos in the world that the average person is more likely to remember a name rather than a logo.

Some people say that they do not have a brand. If you think that you do not have a brand, this is not actually true. Most people that have had some interaction with the Internet in any weight, shape or form, do have an online profile – they already have a brand. It is up to you to control and to shape that brand into exactly what you would want for it to be.

Many people think that they are the kind of people who do not need to have an online personal brand. This is not true. The Internet is excessively powerful and everyone needs to have a stake in this powerful tool. You do not need to share every photo of your latest vacation, or tweet about the last time you went to the washroom or even divulge your tax information online. Simply having a presence online and being the owner of your online brand is enough.

There are many people who think that they are already branded online and they cannot change what has been done. This is not true. With the Internet – if you post something different that would focus on your personal brand and what you want other people to know about you and you were to post this every single day, within three months, you would have completely changed your personal brand online.

Many people love their online personal brand and they think in the classic cliché terms of "if it is not broke, then do not fix it." Well, I would say that I agree with this, however, it does mean that you can neglect to continue to work on maintaining your great online personal brand. It is kind of like losing weight. In order to maintain the weight loss, you must at least continue to keep up with your exercise. The same is true of a great personal online brand. In order to maintain it, even increase it and make it better, you must keep up with it.

There are those people who believe that their credentials stand for themselves. This may be very true, however, unless you start letting the world online know about these great credentials, the people who know about your great credentials will truly be quite an insular circle of people around you. There may be someone whom you graduated with from Oxford University who is sitting by a computer in Greenland that had no idea that you are now a professor at Oxford University. This old school chum of yours would love to find out and get in touch with you. The contact could lead to added research interests on your part. This is just one example of the benefits of touting your own horn to the world.

Others say that online and personal branding makes us less human. This book disagrees with that, however, will consider that point. There are many people who connect locally online and meet up all of the time. Actually, there is a website that is in Canada called Meet Up. The sole purpose of that website is to act as a social media channel for people to build profiles and connect and meet in person in order to get away from the distancing that social media could create if allowed. Online personal branding can be the beginning or the development of many wonderful human interactions, plus interactions with some great animals too. There are many people who find their pets through online as well.

Although this section has addressed some of the misconceptions surrounding online personal branding, there are still some challenges concerning launching and maintaining a successful online personal brand. The next chapter will discuss the challenges of creating and sustaining a successful online personal brand.

Challenges of Personal Branding

This section will discuss the challenges of personal branding. After this chapter it will help you to feel more confident about how to move forward with creating your online personal brand, or also to sustain and maintain your existing online personal brand.

The first step to successful personal branding is again discussed by Peters (1997) in *Fast Company* where it is highly recommended that you take a close look at yourself in your own mirror and assess who you are and what you want you to want to show about which you are through online personal branding. Social media platforms such as LinkedIn, Twitter, Facebook, Instagram and others all reveal an aspect to the world of who you are, so the challenge is to show what you want to show to the world.

In order to do a great job with your personal branding, it is recommended by Peters (1997) that you write out a statement about what you want to show to the world through online personal branding. Peters (1997) recommends as well that this statement that you write out should not be longer than fifteen words. You should be able to answer the questions of how you define yourself, in what way do you want to be viewed as for fame, and once this is established you also have the challenge of staying the course and keeping track of the personal brand that you have established. Just as most people do not really like to see drastic changes in other people, making drastic changes through your online personal branding is also a difficult thing to achieve and will hurt your public profile, depending on the nature of the change.

In many ways, in this section, this is the time to look at what famous and accomplished celebrity figures do with their online personal branding. Whether it is in the area of politics, the area of entertainment and/or sports or people such as Bill Gates, the creator of Microsoft, and Mark Zuckerberg, the creator of Facebook, their online personal branding gets them talked about in positive ways most of the time. This is something that you should aim to strive for in whatever capacity or level that you can.

Another challenge to online personal branding also comes with issues of what photographs to put online. Remember what was said earlier that there could be potential employers and other important people searching you through Google. You must be careful with the kinds of photographs that you put online. Photos of you drunk at the office party at the nearby banquet hall may not look very appealing to a potential employer and/or a potential client.

You must remember that the concept of online personal branding is also an aspect of public relations (PR). Through social media, you now have the power to be your own PR person and you can shape who you want to be online, an authentic representation of your best self. So, who do you want to be? What do you want the public to see? This is essentially the challenge and we will touch on this topic again throughout this book, even in the next chapter.

The next chapter tackles the question, what are the biggest challenges of branding? This will help you to prepare to launch your online personal branding soon, as well as to prepare you to jump over any hurdles of obstacles that may arise as you are creating or sustaining your online personal brand.

What Are The Biggest Challenges Of Branding?

This section of the book discusses and answers the question, what are the biggest challenges of branding? Once you have read this chapter, you will have a clearer insight into exactly what you need to do to have a successful online profile, a successful online brand.

There are many challenges when it comes to developing your own personal branding. If you are starting out with an online personal brand for the first time and find that when you Google yourself that there are not many things said about you online and yet, there is much you have done that you would want the world to know about, one of the first things that this book suggests is that you consider starting a blog site.

Most blog sites are free and you can start posting things that are of interest to you. If you are politically minded, you can express some of your political views, however, make sure that you are getting the points across that you want that will not harm your reputation. As well, if you own a business, you can incorporate a blog into the website so that not only will you rank higher in Google, but you will also receive more customers, clients, and business for your entity.

As mentioned before, it can take about three months to rank your own name in the top of Google. Some of the challenges to ranking at the top of Google would be if you have a name such as John Smith. John Smith is a common name for the people who would have access to the Internet. You may want to consider using a middle name or some kind of title and/or suffix that is attached to your name in order to set yourself apart with your personal online branding.

The same goes for your business name. There are sometimes other businesses that exist on the worldwide web that have the same business name that you would have. If you are just starting a business, one of the ways to get around having difficulties with similar business names that works great for entrepreneurs is to simply use your own unique name to name your company.

Another obstacle that comes up with online personal branding is that you need to make sure that if you do create a blog that it is one that is connected with such social media platforms as LinkedIn, Twitter, Facebook, Instagram, Google+ and others. This way, each time that you make a post, all of your connections will see it.

This also brings up another obstacle. You must make sure that you are actively involved in connecting with people online. There is the risk that you could end up connecting with the wrong person and mayhem could occur from everything from this person that you connect with disrespecting you online and/or a situation such as fraud occurring. The way to get around this is to ensure that the connections that you make are linked through other people that you know and then this should ideally create connections which are formed based on healthy relationships ensuring that your online personal branding situation will be a healthy one.

The next chapter in this book is an important one. This chapter will discuss some of the mistakes to avoid when it comes to online personal branding. Please read this chapter carefully because it will help to ensure that your experience of your online personal brand will be more positive than negative.

Personal Branding Mistakes

This section will discuss some of the personal online branding mistakes to avoid as you are on your online personal branding journey. Reading this chapter will help you to have a more enjoyable journey on the pathway of the online personal journey. Kind of like taking your favourite music with you on a road trip rather than listening to whatever station is on the radio that you may not like.

Make sure number one that you are careful about what you say online. If you say something that will upset many people, this could ruin not only your personal reputation but also the reputation of your business if this is one of your motivations to brand yourself online.

Another aspect to consider is to be careful of the photographs that you put online. As mentioned before, you may not want to show off how great you think you look in your bathing suit in the summertime at the beach no matter what your partner has told you about how beautiful you look as just one example. Such aspects of nudity online may be a little bit too revealing for a potential client and/or a potential employer.

Another thing to keep in mind when you are online is to ensure that if you are in a chat session through a portal such as Twitter, make sure that if you are following the conversation that you have actually read what is going on and that you are thoughtfully responding to the information that you are receiving. The same goes for Facebook. This will ensure that you will also develop a great online presence as a good listener.

The famous American hip-hop singer Beyoncé once said in one of her songs, "I ain't gonna diss you on the Internet because my Mama taught me better than that." Whether you enjoy Beyoncé's music or not, those lines are ones that everyone who is into developing a healthy image of them online should live by. If someone happens to attack you online, the best advice that this book could give is to simply not respond to it. If other people online ask you why you are not responding, simply let them know that you do not respond to such public displays of anger and that the action was not called for. Once word gets around regarding the way you responded and the way the other person responded – you will come out the winner in the end, particularly when social graces are considered.

Another really bad mistake to do online is to not be you. There are many situations of illegal child luring for dating purposes and other purposes and all kinds of things that people will do that are illegal when they are not being honest about who they are online.

Know the law and know that you are expected to be who you are online and not someone else, whether this other person is real or not. The only time that is allowed is in computer gaming and usually, the real player is identifiable. So, please, know the law and avoid this at all costs.

Make sure that when you are dealing with people online that you ask the toughest questions first! This could be a great prevention from online fraud or any illegal online activity to say the least, or even from getting a client that you do not want and/or as a customer yourself, not getting the goods and the services that you want.

Another mistake that some people do online is taking too long to respond to people that try to contact them. Try to make every effort to respond to people within a reasonable period of time. Months should not need to go by until someone hears a response from you. This will give you a bad reputation.

Now that we have discussed the mistakes to avoid with online personal branding, we will next discuss the importance of online personal branding. This will help to reinforce what you are embarking on and to keep you motivated. You may need to read this chapter many times while you are conducting the start of your online personal brand, and/or sustaining your existing online personal brand.

Importance of Personal Branding

This chapter is important. Not just because it has the word "important" in it, but also because of this chapter, if you read it more than once, has the potential to keep you motivated as you start, and continue your journey with online personal branding. The next chapter is also important as well.

As mentioned in earlier sections of this book, people are usually drawn to developing an online brand because they care about their image to the world. They care about the digital footprint that will leave on the Internet after they leave this world. They want the good things that they are known for to be known to the world. They have a product and or service that they want to build more clients for and they know that personal online branding will help with this. Most importantly out of all of this, they care about their reputations and this is probably the sum total of all of the reasons why people desire to have a strong online personal presence.

The first question to ask yourself whether you are developing an online personal brand for the first time, or you are assessing your own established online personal brand or anywhere in between those two spectrums is, how important is your personal reputation to you?

If your answer to this question is: "it is very important to me," then automatically you understand the importance of online personal branding.

The importance of online personal branding is no different than in the days of yore when many people would not discuss certain things in public and among their respected colleagues because they feared that discussing such things would hurt their reputations.

Nowadays, things have changed. Many people who speak out against such issues around the world as child soldiers in countries which civil war, bad treatment to animals, human trafficking and child trafficking, poverty, hunger, disease, and the plights of the world are actually applauded for speaking out and bringing attention to such matters to a worldwide audience through online personal branding.

Others nowadays, they are applauded for innovative ideas in science, technology, the arts, sports, medicine, real estate, education and many other fields. Online personal branding is not just important because the world gets to know you, but also because the world gets to know about what you care about the most.

The next chapter is similar to this chapter where it can keep you motivated on your online personal branding journey through the discussion of the benefits of online personal branding.

Benefits of Personal Branding

The benefits of online personal branding are the topic of this section of the book.

This chapter will become important to you as well in order to keep you motivated on the online personal branding journey.

The benefits of online personal branding are that you have a vehicle in which to express your thoughts and your ideas and your passions. Not only do you have a vehicle in which to express your thoughts and your ideas and your passions – you have the great opportunity to share all of these wonderful things with the rest of world who are connected to the Internet. You will not be alone on the worldwide web – this is for sure.

Online personal branding done beautifully is a full expression of you. You are allowed to be yourself. As long as you are abiding by the laws and regulations of the place in which you live, the country where you live and the worldwide protocols, there is nothing stopping you from even creating something really new and different that is an idea that you have been incubating in your mind and in notebooks for perhaps even decades and then sharing these ideas with the vast and great audience of the worldwide web.

It is not uncommon that people who participate in online personal branding begin to gain the great benefit of increased confidence and feeling more vital and important. It feels great to connect with new and interesting people on daily basis and have conversations from London, England with people who are in Malaysia right from the comfort of your desktop, laptop, and/or mobile device. In any given day, not only can you travel the world and meet interesting people, you can also find a client in South America who have been waiting anxiously to find someone such as you in order to purchase your product and/or service.

With the power of the Internet, even if you are a "big cheese" in your field offline, the Internet will give you more credibility and a wider network of people in order to build your career, your franchise and/or your business.

Another great benefit of online personal branding is leaving your own positive distinguished mark on the worldwide web and the powerful entity of a platform that is the Internet, potentially for even centuries after you have passed away.

For business purposes, building your online personal brand is a great way to target your audience for your audience for your goods and services. You will reach the customer base that you want and increase your profit margin.

Online personal branding also helps to carve out a niche for yourself in the competitive marketplace of businesses that will be your own. By being yourself, you automatically distinguish yourself from the competition and those customers who like you and like what you do will buy from you.

If you are looking for someone to support a project that you are working on or just even for some sponsorship of a business initiative that you have, the Internet and online is a great way to do get the support you need. It could even be something on a personal level such as getting rid of an addiction that you have such as drinking and/or smoking cigarettes. The online community has plenty of support groups to help with that. As well, so you are looking to lose weight, or improve your cooking skills, or even know how to drive a car and gain the confidence to get out there on the road – building your online personal brand will help to draw to you people who can help you on whatever path in life that you need support

Online personal branding is also a great way to concentrate and to focus the energy that you have and to use towards productive and profitable purposes.

Another benefit of online personal branding is that it an activity that is extremely cost-effective when it comes to promoting either yourself and/or your business. If you desire to promote your business, creating a profile on LinkedIn, Facebook, Instagram, Twitter, Google+ and other social media networks online costs nothing at all. Connecting with people online also costs nothing at all. If you choose to have some of the premium services that are offered with LinkedIn, Facebook, Instagram, Twitter, Google+ and other social media networks, the cost is minimal. You can even pay, for a minimal fee, to have advertisements on Facebook, and also with Google AdWords as just two examples. All of this will help to promote your business, plus your online personal branding. There are other online television portals such as YouTube.com and ThatChannel.com where to advertise on these sites is at a very low fee, sometimes as low as thirty dollars per month in Canadian currency.

The most important thing about online personal branding – who would you be more likely to give your last dollar to if they asked? Would you give it to a homeless person that you met in the emergency room when a baby is being born and they entertained you with stories of them riding the trains through Paris? Or, would you give it to some faceless company that has not ever said thank you to you for paying your bills on time for the last twenty years? Think about it. People give money to people – not companies. This is another important reason why online personal branding is so vital.

The next chapter will discuss the elements of online personal branding.

Elements of Your Personal Brand

This section discusses what are the key elements that need to be comprised of your online personal brand?

The very first priority is developing, building and maintaining an online personality. As mentioned before, this is best developed through blogs. As well, the photos that you use for yourself, as well as when you change your photos and also how often you change your photographs online and the number of different photographs that you have online will also develop your online personality. Another aspect of developing an online personality is also the use of video and audio as well, as well as the strength of your own writing when text needs to be used. If you have any challenges with any of things, it would be recommended that you consider hiring experts in these fields to help you to build the best online personal branding that you can.

The second priority, particularly if you own a business is that your company needs to have a mission statement and a set of values that it follows. There are many people out there that are only looking to do business with those companies which they consider socially responsible. By socially responsible meaning that they want to give their money to companies that are not simply looking at the bottom line in terms of making money, but are also concerned about treating their employees well, giving back to society and making some kind of important difference in the world.

It's important that you authentically and truthfully express what interests you and what your passions are through online personal branding. You may feel shy to do so, however, you would be amazed how many people are out there that agree with you wholeheartedly. Would you not want to connect with these people and fuel more positive energy into your passions and interests?

A lot of successful online personal branding is about focusing on your strengths. What are you really good? What can you boast about? What could you also do to help others because you are so good at it?

Another key element of your personal brand includes your work experience as well as your educational experience. There are many people that would want to connect with you just because you have gone to the same school and/or you have worked at the same organizations. The same is true of the organizations you tend to follow online. There are many people who would want to follow you on Twitter because of who you follow.

In this chapter as well, we will discuss some elements of your personal brand in terms of written communication that would also be helpful in developing your online personal brand depending on the industry that you work in.

Government Communications

When it comes to government communications there are some key things government professionals use to get their work done. They are the following:

- Media Advisories
- News Releases
- Backgrounders
- Fact Sheets
- Media Qs and As
- Speeches

Media Advisories

There are standard formats when it comes to media advisories. The purpose of a media advisory is to let the media know of an event happening within the government the media may want to cover.

Different from news releases, these advisories simply state the basic information of the event, answering the key questions such as:

- Who is holding the event?
- When is it taking place?
- Where is it taking place?
- Why is it taking place?
- Plus potentially how it could be covered?

These advisories simply have the nuts and bolts.

Media Releases

Different from advisories, you would actually write more detail into a media release which may also include quotes from notable people who are important behind releasing the information – the movers and shakers if you will.

Some online personal branders will re-write a media release and publish that or broadcast it. You need to make sure the quality of the release is publishable, clear, has contact information so journalists can follow with further questions and may also include information of possible visuals which can be used in a television story.

When writing you would want to paint pictures with your words, use plain language (which is an important movement in the government). They are increasingly moving away from bureaucratic language. Having a corporate writing background is definitely an asset to the government.

Backgrounders

Another important government communication product is the backgrounder. This is often important to give to media because on issues such as the Walkerton water scandal which happened a few years ago – the media may need to have background information they can use in their story.

Doing backgrounders requires research and you would want to lay out the information in such a way it's clear to journalists what the background on the story actually is. The Communication Guide for the government has an outline which clearly demonstrates the required formats for such things as backgrounders, media advisories, news releases and fact sheets that we'll talk about next.

Fact Sheets

Fact sheets are important in such situations as looking at employment rates in Ontario, as an example, which can clearly outline some of the facts behind a story.

Again, there are standard formats which the government uses.

Okay...here are eight tips on improving your writing:

1. Passive verbs: the subject of the sentence appears to be receiving, rather than doing, the action – for example: "The cake was baked by the father." Instead try: "Father baked the cake."

2. Verbs Turned into Nouns: a common error – "It's my understanding that..." Try instead: "I understand that..."

3. Pretentious words: "We are required to purchase." Try instead: "We need to buy."

4. Unnecessary words: "The program is currently in need of help." Rather, "The program needs help."

5. Noun chains: nouns proceeded by two or more adjectives, such as: "expenditure management guidelines." "Guidelines on managing expenditures."

6. Words unfamiliar to your audience: strategic coherence; input validation; re-engineering.

7. Lack of variety: A new program has been announced. This program promises to be a program we can all be proud of. Rather, "our ministry is launching a new program.

It promises to be one we can still all be proud of."

8. Run-on sentences and paragraphs: sentences longer than 25 words. After that, readers start to forget what they've read and have to re-read. Also, paragraphs longer than three sentences.

Keep in mind in government communications, if your audience can read your document quickly and understand it the first time around, you have succeeded.

Marketing   Explained

1. You're a woman and you see a handsome guy at a party. You go up to him and say, "I'm fantastic in bed."
   That's Direct Marketing.

2. You're at a party with a bunch of friends and see a handsome guy. One of your friends goes up to him and, pointing at you, says, "She's fantastic in bed."
   That's Advertising.

3. You see a handsome guy at a party. You go up to him and get his telephone number. The next day you call and say, "Hi, I'm fantastic in bed."
   That's Telemarketing.

4. You see a guy at a party; you straighten your dress. You walk up to him and pour him a drink. You say, "May I?" and reach up to straighten his tie, brushing your breast lightly against his arm, and then say: "By the way, I'm fantastic in bed."
   That's Public Relations.

5. You're at a party and see a handsome guy. He walks up to you and says, "I hear you're fantastic in bed."
   That's Brand Recognition.

6. You're at a party and see a handsome guy. He fancies you, but you talk him into going home with your friend.

That's a Sales Rep.

7. Your friend can't satisfy him so he calls you.
    That's Tech Support.

8. You're on your way to a party when you realize that there could be handsome men
    in all these houses you're passing., so you climb onto the roof of one situated
    towards the centre and shout at the top of your lungs, "I'm fantastic in bed!"
    That's Junk Mail.

9. You are at a party; this well-built man walks up to you and grabs your ass.
    That's Former President Clinton.

10. You like it, but twenty years later your attorney decides you were offended.
    That's America.

Presentations

When it comes to doing online performances with your online personal branding,
here are some tips with working with audio-visual elements of your online personal
branding. You may get invited or seek out to do a TED Talk online and you need to be
prepared. Doing a TED Talk would certainly help to raise your online personal brand and
show other people what you are passionate about. However, you could also create your
own through YouTube.com or through ThatChannel.com.

Here are some points I'd like to share:

- Try to write an outline. It is the best tool for setting a solid foundation from which to
  build the other parts of the presentation.
- Clear, logical organization of ideas has a major impact on the effectiveness of a
  presentation.
- Define your objectives and the message you want to give the audience. Do you
  want to inform, explain, persuade, inspire, or entertain?
- Focus on your audiences' needs and design your presentation accordingly.
- Break the talk into an introduction, body, and summary to isolate the needs of each
  presentation stage. By tackling each part separately, you can address the specific
  needs of each phase and ensure key messages are not overlooked.
- Bolt down the dozen or so ideas you want to talk about to three or four essential
  ideas to establish key segments you must discuss.

- Often, making a few background comments on your topic to bring everyone "up to speed" is very useful.
- The most interesting and effective presentations generally include a substantial amount of well-chosen forms of support such as analogies, examples, statistical data and references. The most effective supporting material is relevant, accurate, and appropriate and put in terms the audience will understand, respect and respond to.
- In reefing the presentation, write all key points and sub-points as complete, simple sentences. This clarifies ideas and aids testing for logical connection of ideas.
- If you are using visual aids, use a storyboard to match the oral and visual elements. Try to keep the content of your flipcharts, overhead transparencies, slides, or computer graphics to:
    1. six lines or bullets per page;
    2. three to five words per line;
    3. The smallest letter should be visible by the most distant viewer.

Step three: Testing and Rehearsing

What are some of the things you think needs to be done to properly test and rehearse a presentation?

Those are good ideas.

Here are some points I'd like to add:

- Testing, rehearsing and polishing prepare you for possible problems and does wonder for self-confidence.
- Practice your speech out loud to hear how it sounds to your own ear.
- Change any phrases or words that are giving you trouble. Your presentation should reflect your personal style.
- Make notes on the delivery copy of your presentation. If you feel you are always going too fast in a particular section or not emphasizing or smiling enough, mark "SLOW HERE," EMPHASIZE HERE," "PAUSE HERE," or "SMILE HERE" in the margins.
- Conduct a dry run before a good friend or colleague. Practice is nine-tenths of the way toward achieving an effective presentation. Yet practice without evaluation is an inefficient use of time and limited in its potential for improvement.

- Ask the friend or colleague for honest feedback. An objective observer can often spot gaps or shaky points in a presentation more quickly than the presenter, who may be too close to the issue.
- Dry runs also help to check the length of the material and its delivery time, since presenters often miscalculate the amount of material they can cover in the allotted time.
- As well, dry runs usually improve the fluency of the presenter. It prevents embarrassment as it helps you to catch glitches in your visual support materials, such as misspelled words. A speaker should consider all comments, and incorporate changes where feasible and desirable.

O.K. now we'll move onto step four.

Step four: Delivery and show time

What are some of the things you think needs to be done for delivery and show time of the presentation?

Here are some things I'd like to note too about delivery and show time:

- Arrive early at the venue. Check all equipment and visual aids in advance.
- After you are introduced, walk slowly to the podium. Adopt a comfortable stance, pause and let the room come to order. Then, thank the person who introduced you, look people in their eyes and smile.
- Your opening lines are especially important to get the show off to a lively start. Do not be afraid to put some feeling into your presentation. Speakers who have a high degree of vocal expressiveness are better able to get their message across.
- Speak slowly and clearly. Don't rush through your script or notes.
- However, audiences do appreciate and need occasional changes of pace, Different concepts require different treatments.
- Describing a technical point, for example, needs more deliberate care and repetition than reviewing o something that is familiar to the audience. Listeners often attribute thoughtfulness to a speaker when he or she changes to a more deliberate manner. Use silence following a key point to let it sink in.
- Basically, you voice should be:
    1. loud enough to be heard;
    2. clear enough to be understood;
    3. expressive enough to be interesting'
    4. Pleasing enough to be enjoyable.

- If you are reading from a script, start to read aloud with your eyes down. Scan to the end of the sentence (or a phrase, if it's a long sentence).
- Look up and deliver this portion of the text to the audience. Pause. Look down and continue.
- Non-verbal behaviour can send a message all its own. No matter what your words say or how they sound, your body may communication something very different.
- Eye contact is critical. Look at individual members, not at the group as a whole. Make eye contact for two to three seconds; don't scan the group or start at people. Avoid focusing on one side of the room or on key audience members. This applies to groups of six or six hundred.
- Avoid distracting movements such as jiggling coins in your pocket (better yet, take the coins out of your pocket), playing with your hair, scratching an imaginary (or real) itch, or fiddling with jewelry or clothing. Many of these habits are exaggerated when you are nervous.
- Use your hands for emphasis and illustration. Focus on the individuals in your audience, and forget about your hands.
- If you can't forget your hands, try this: Hold your hands, elbows bent, at waist level. Lightly touch the thumb of one hand to the ring finger of the other. Relax your fingers. Your hands are now ready to move or gesture as you need them.

We'll also discuss more spokespeople as working as one as soon as we're done with step five.

Step five: Handling feedback

How do you think you would handle feedback?

- During the question and answer phase, actively list to the question. Let the questioner know you are interested in looking at the questioner, nodding your head or showing other facial expressions.
- If you do not understand the question, ask the questioner to clarify or reword it. If the question is a hostile one, rephrase it for the audience, removing any hostile words or tone.
- Respond to the question. If you do not have a complete answer, say so. Seek further information from the audience, or commit to getting an answer following the presentation.
- When you have completed your response, check back with the questioner to make sure you have given the information that he or she was seeking.

- If the question was a hostile one, does not check back but move on to the next questioner?

Here are some last minute tips:

It is natural to be nervous before presentations. Here are some suggestions to help you control your apprehension.

- Give yourself plenty of time to arrive at the venue. A last minute dash will leave you breathless and with no time to check the equipment and the facility. Such uncertainties will increase your nervousness.
- Take some deep breaths to clear your head and to get your breathing under control. If you can get somewhere private for a moment, try tensing all your muscles and then letting them relax.
- Look people directly in the eyes. If you are nervous, look for the friendly faces. Move your gaze to various people in all parts of the room but avoid a jerky, shifty look.
- Think positive. You are likely to know more about this subject than most people in your audience. You have prepared and have interesting information to give to them. If you believe that (and it's true), it will increase your confidence.
- Keep your perspective. Don't take the presentation too seriously. Try to enjoy it, if you do, your audience will too.

This chapter has discussed the importance of the elements of personal branding. The next chapter will discuss who should be building an online personal brand.

Who should be Building a Personal Brand?

If you do not think online personal branding is for you – well, it is for everyone.

If you are a boss, online personal branding can be a great way for your employees to get to know you, as well as to understand your work ethics for your employees to follow, plus build relationships and conversation topics with everyone who works for your businesses. Bosses that are looking to rise to the ranks to higher in their businesses, online personal branding can be a great way in which to do so if you craft your online profile carefully and strategically.

The same goes for employees of an organization. Whether you are looking for employment or not, a great online personal brand for yourself will draw potential employers to you, plus help to raise the public profile of your company that just may result in you getting a much-needed raise.

Unemployed people could just find the job of their dreams through a strong online personal brand. Particularly if someone who is unemployed is willing to travel to other parts of the world in order to receive employment, this book can almost guarantee that you will find a job on this planet in a matter than no more than one month through successful online personal branding. One of the most important skill sets that it shows to potential employers is that you know how to use the Internet and computers well.

Entrepreneurs and small business people can gain many clients through online personal branding. This is a great way to increase your profit margin and almost expect an increase in business year after year the more you increase your online branded presence.

Students are in a great position in order to increase their online personal brand. Not only would online personal branding help them to get a job right out of school, it is also beneficial for students to connect with other students either locally, nationally or internationally in order to seek out avenues for further study after they graduate if they desire to do so.

The Do's and Don'ts of Personal Branding

This section will discuss the do's and don'ts of online personal branding.

Do:

- **Use the active voice whenever possible. For example: "I am happy," rather than "I was happy." Most things online have a date attached to it so it will make for more interesting reading if you keep everything in the active voice.**

- Make sure that you tell stories to the world that interest you and other people that you have told the stories to.

- Do show your passion!

- If you know something has a strong reputation and you are associated with it – piggyback on that reputation and make sure to "drop the name" so-to-speak when you are connecting with other people online and in your blogs.

- Make sure the whole world knows your mission statement and your values.

- Try to make a new potential client at least once per day.

- Do your research! If there is something online that you do not know about, check it out when you are in doubt!

Don't:

- Do not speak of yourself as being a brand through your online personal branding. This tends to turn people off.

- Try to avoid catchphrases. Come up with fresh and new statements. Challenge yourself to be new and unique.

- As mentioned before with the Beyoncé song, do not "diss" anyone on the Internet.

- If you are talking about yourself, try to include other people as well. You do not want to come across as arrogant.

- Keep coming up with new ideas to express to the world at least once a week. Do not go months without attending to your online personal branding. Your profiles will get stale and you will lose your Google ranking.

- If you do not have a connection with a company, do not mention it no matter how big it is.

Developing Your Personal Brand

This section will focus on how to develop a strong online personal brand. The goals of developing a strong online personal brand are as follows:

- To establish a strong image of yourself online.
- To connect with key people in your industry and/or client-base that will help with the profits of your company.
- To connect with key people who can support your business efforts and any projects that you want to undertake.
- To rank high in Google under your personal name and your personal brand.
- To have good things said about you online.
- To generate strong reviews from others regarding your goods and services associated with your online personal brand.

The ways to do this are as follows.

To establish a strong image of you online:

The ways of establishing a strong image of you online are through the process of having attractive photographs of yourself online. If you are not in possession of these photographs, it would be highly advisable that you hire a professional photographer in order to take these photographs.

As well, having a blog can help you to establish your credibility online. If your writing skills are not what you would want them to be, hire a professional writer to help you with this aspect as well.

Adding video and audio are also great options for establishing your online personal branding. All of this can also be done on many social media sites such as LinkedIn, Twitter, Instagram, Facebook, Google+, and many other social media sites.

To connect with key people in your industry and/or client-base that will help with the profits of your company:

Once you have established your strong online personal profiles, you must start making targeted efforts to connect with those people online that you want to connect with. As a rule of thumb when it comes to Twitter, try to only follow those people who will also follow you. Once you have your blog that will broadcast out to various social media platforms that you are linked with, you will also gain a following through your blog as well.

To connect with key people who can support your business efforts and any projects that you want to undertake:

Another aspect of connecting with people online is to connect with potential business clients and personal clients that will help you to increase your profits with business through your online personal branding. Search these people out, or, you may already know of people that you would want to connect with. Connecting with them is just a computer and a click away.

To rank high in Google under your personal name and your personal brand:

Your ranking on Google is determined on how often you post online. This is why blogging is one of the best ways to increase your ranking with Google. If you post at least daily, if not even more than once per day and you are just starting out – no doubts at all that within three months you will see a significant presence of your own personal name at least on the front page of Google when your search for your name as was mentioned at the beginning of this book.

To have good things said about you online:

In order to have good things said about you online, encourage your friends and clients to comment positively about you online. This will increase your online profile reputation and create a positive online personal branding presence.

To generate strong reviews from others regarding your goods and services associated with your online personal brand:

Also associated with having people say good things about you online, have your customers leave great reviews about you online. If your services can facilitate a survey as well that will help you to improve your business, send out a Survey Monkey which you can find online in order to assess how your clients think and view your business and post the comments on your blog and/or your website.

The Power of the Written World with Elements of Online Personal Branding

Using the example of an online personal branding campaign that would help to stop young people from drinking underage, here is an example below:

Alcohol as Image: Since the ancient Greeks celebrated Dionysus, the god of wine, theater, and ecstasy, a connection has endured among alcohol, media, and sensuality. In addition to sharing a profound appeal to the senses, alcohol, theater, and ecstasy offer an escape from the mundane and a sense of liberation. The view of intoxication as a celebration and a rite of passage continues to this day, anchored by the many messages modern society reflects in its depictions of alcohol through advertising.

Echoes of Dionysus reverberate throughout much modern advertising for alcohol, which often touts youth, sexual prowess, beauty, and athleticism. Initiation into manhood, quite often involving male bonding through modern-day sporting events, is rarely viewed as complete without alcohol. Alcohol advertisers carefully create their own myths about alcohol normalcy, portraying the world where the successful people drink and all drinkers are rewarded.

Through advertising, young people, in particular, learn to associate alcohol with social acceptance. Those who abstain are promptly left behind and dismissed. Young people are especially susceptible to the lure of alcohol advertising. The images depicting alcohol's social benefits are wildly exaggerated and distorted by alcohol advertising, and many young people tend to accept the misconception that drinking will somehow improve their lives.

Instead of finding the advertised camaraderie and companionship, many will find themselves, years later, abusing alcohol alone. Alcohol advertising frequently sells one reality but delivers another.

Alcohol Advertising and Youth: The legal age to buy alcohol in all fifty US states is twenty-one years. Many people argue that some alcohol advertising campaigns are designed specifically to appeal to the youth market, despite the legal barriers to consumption. One such compelling argument was frequently made about the advertising mascot Spuds McKenzie, a highly appealing 1980s ad image of a bull terrier dog, the original "party animal."

Wearing sunglasses, a bandana, a Hawaiian shirt, and headphones, and holding a Bud Light beer, Spuds was depicted in tropical locales and surrounded by beautiful, scantily clad young women. First appearing to acclaim in a 1987 Bud Light commercial during the broadcast of the Super Bowl, Spuds, throughout the late 1980s, rode skateboards, raced horses, drove convertibles, maneuvered surfboards, played Frisbee, and combed beaches.

Sales of Bud Light beer soared during the Spuds ad campaign, which not only marketed the alcoholic beverage but also sold millions of dollars of Spuds paraphernalia: everything from T-shirts to caps to plush toys. Anti-drinking groups responded by arguing that the campaign targeted children and teenagers. In 1989, Mothers against Drunk

Driving claimed that Anheuser-Busch, the maker of Bud Light, was deceptively marketing alcohol to children and demanded that Spuds ads cease promoting the beer. An investigation of the ad campaign by the Federal Trade Commission (FTC) ensued, and although the FTC found no wrongdoing by Anheuser-Busch, the company nevertheless terminated the campaign in 1989.

Anheuser-Busch again ignited controversy in the 1990s with its Budweiser Frogs ad campaign. First appearing in a Super Bowl television commercial in 1995, the Budweiser Frogs depicted three frogs, Bud, Weis, and Er, who lived on a log in a swamp behind a bar and croaked "Budweiser" rhythmically. In 1996, a study revealed that considerable numbers of nine- to eleven-year-old children could easily identify the Budweiser Frogs and associate them with beer, but was unable to recognize or identify various children's cartoon figures. Anti-drinking groups again accused the alcohol industry of targeting children.

Shortly thereafter, another study revealed that when asked to name US presidents, most eight- to twelve-year-old children could name few but had no difficulty naming a variety of brands of beer. In spite of these negative reports, the Budweiser Frogs campaign continued for many years; it is recognized in the adverting industry as one of most successful marketing campaigns in history.

A 2015 study published in *JAMA Pediatrics* found that exposure to alcohol ads predicted the onset of underage drinking as well as binge and hazardous drinking in young people between the ages of fifteen and twenty-three. However, the same year, a study from the University of Texas at Austin found that while alcohol advertising increased 400% between 1971 and 2011, overall alcohol sales did not do so significantly, suggesting a weaker link between advertising and alcohol consumption.

Alcohol and Sporting Events: The alcohol industry is a frequent sponsor and promoter of sporting events, many of which appeal to a large percentage of fans who are minors. From the Super Bowl to the World Series to auto racing to college basketball, the alcohol industry spends billions of sponsorship and advertising dollars each year, specifically targeting an audience of sports fans, many of them younger than twenty-one years.

The alcohol industry provides a lucrative source of funding for collegiate sports, especially the National Collegiate Athletic Association's (NCAA) annual basketball championships (known as March Madness), but some critics argue that the price for this funding is too high, owing to the toll it levies in the form of underage drinking. The NCAA's playoff and championship games, for instance, welcome millions of children and minors as viewers each year, who are subjected to the same degree of intense alcohol advertising as adults. Although the alcohol industry maintains that it is advertising its products so rigorously during such sporting events only to establish brand loyalty among adults who already drink, March Madness nonetheless draws millions of underage viewers.

According to the National Institute on Alcohol Abuse and Alcoholism (NIAAA), studies reveal a greater propensity among young people to initiate drinking at a younger age if they are heavily exposed to alcohol advertising. Moreover, the NIAAA cites evidence demonstrating that the younger a person begins to drink, the greater the likelihood that he or she will become an alcoholic. For example, statistically, the NIAAA reports that a person who begins drinking by age fifteen years is four times as likely to become a heavy drinker and dependent on alcohol as a person who begins drinking at age twenty-one years.

Children, drawn to watch their favorite sports teams and athletes, are ill-equipped to decipher the deceptive messages of alcohol advertising. Youths often come away from watching such sporting competitions with a false sense of normalcy, believing that alcohol consumption as portrayed by advertising is ubiquitous, harmless, fun, and inconsequential, regardless of age or circumstance. Fans attending both collegiate and professional sporting events sponsored by alcohol companies have recently become increasingly dismayed and alarmed at the escalation of public drunkenness and violence occurring among fans, an environment that is growing increasingly unsafe for children.

The above is an example of the kind of online personal branding that would be involved with a social media campaign against underage drinking.

The Power of Your Voice with Audio-Visual Elements of Online Personal Branding

Your voice is your most powerful tool. Think of actors such as Dustin Hoffman, Barbara Streisand, and Jim Carey. These actors are not the prettiest people in the world. They have terrific voices. One way to supercharge your blog, website, or even your online profiles on Twitter, Facebook, LinkedIn, Instagram and any form of social media are to create podcasts of your voice through these social media vehicles. There are also many social media platforms such as Podomatic.com which is completely devoted to the showcasing of podcasts. Podcasts are similar to having a radio show. You can have interesting radio shows concerning the daily operations of your business. You can have interesting radio shows to bring sound to elements that you write either on your blog and/or website. Sound can make a great difference and for those people who cannot see online because of site problems, you will also be branching out to an element of the population that you normally would not be able to reach if you did not add sound to your online personal branding.

The Power of Your Face with Audio-Visual Elements of Online Personal Branding

Through online video portals such as YouTube.com, Vimeo.com, and others such as ThatChannel.com, you can add your face and words and create an engaging video for your online personal branding. All of this helps people to know exactly who you are, what you believe in and to make you more of a real person so if they want to buy from you if your incentive is financial reasons for business – they will do so depending on what you say. If people like what you say and like what you have to offer in terms of your business and its special uniqueness and what it can give to them, you are developing a strong online personal brand.

The next chapter involves using social media for online personal branding. This chapter is an interesting one so please keep reading.

.

Using Social Media for Personal Branding

I am going to begin this chapter with what researchers are saying about the effects that social media has on college students as one example. This portion of this chapter will answer the following questions in one short paragraph for each question. First, I will summarize the research project. My summary should clearly identify the project's research question. I will describe the survey and choice of the sample; and present the results of the project. Second, I will answer what were the strengths of this research project? I will consider both the methodology and the sample selection. For the methodology, I will think about the strengths of the survey research, and whether this project took advantage of those strengths. For sample selection, think about whether the project selected a truly representative sample. Third, I will answer what were the weaknesses of this research project? I will consider both the methodology and the sample selection.

First Question

For a summary of the research, Wang, Chen & Liang (2011) believe that social media is a high priority in the success of college students today. The research results were determined by survey research on a quantitative research methodology scale. The questionnaire that was involved in the research primarily took place at Johnson & Wales University

(Wang, Chen & Liang, 2011). The research results determined that social media sites are a vitally important part of the lives of college students (Wang, Chen & Liang, 2011). The research also determines that there is a negative impact although social media is important, to the use of social media in the lives of college students (Wang, Chen & Liang, 2011). The research question is the effects of social media on college students (Wang, Chen & Liang, 2011).

Second Question

For the methodology, a random survey sample of 48 men and 26 females were given a questionnaire (Wang, Chen & Liang, 2011). The main question that was asked was their perceptions of how they felt social media affected college students (Wang, Chen & Liang, 2011). Out of the respondents, 35% were undergraduate students and 65% of the students were graduate students (Wang, Chen & Liang, 2011). Again, out of the respondents, 31% of the students have employment with full-time jobs, 30% have part-time employment and 39% of the students did not have jobs (Wang, Chen & Liang, 2011). The research results were that 45% of the respondents spend more than six hours a day, sometimes even eight hours a day on social media sites (Wang, Chen & Liang, 2011). The strengths of the survey research are that the questionnaire and research tool was rather comprehensive with a strong sampling of respondents used for this qualitative research (Wang, Chen & Liang, 2011).

Third Question

The weaknesses of this research are that the research was only conducted at one university, that being Johnson & Wales University (Wang, Chen & Liang, 2011). The fact that other universities were not part of this research does not result in a comprehensive assessment of how potentially other students at other universities would be using social media and its effects on them as students (Wang, Chen & Liang, 2011).

In conclusion of this section, it responded to three questions concerning the research of Wang, Chen & Liang (2011). It was determined that although the research efforts were good, that there are also some flaws in the research by the fact that only one university was involved in the assessment process of this research question of the effects of social media on college students.

Here is an example below of a social media campaign.

For this example, using The Rock Insurance case study, we will start developing a Social Media Plan for The Rock Insurance Company. We will develop a final profile of the target customers that The Rock should focus on for the future. We will do Technographic Profile building along with the instructions from the Goldenberg (2015) book. In two to three paragraphs, I will determine whether or not this would be beneficial to The Rock. We will look at how would The Rock set goals for their Social Media campaign? We will define Social Media platforms and how they are used.

Social Media Campaign

For a Social Media Campaign for The Rock Insurance Company, we would first create a LinkedIn profile for the company. We would encourage other people on LinkedIn to follow the company, as well as make connections with some key companies, as well as individuals who would be interested in investing in The Rock Insurance Company. Next, we would create a Twitter account where I would have the newly hired Content Manager/Social Media Manager of The Rock Insurance send news, information and interesting information concerning The Rock Insurance Company's discounts, specials and promotions to everyone that we are connected to on Twitter. Next, we would create a company website on Facebook. On this website, we would also pay for advertising of The Rock Insurance and get people to know more about the company who did not know about it before. Next, we would connect with Google Ads and create an advertising campaign through Google Ads for The Rock Insurance Company.

Target Audience

The target audience that we would set out for The Rock in terms of future clients would be young people. I would also create an app that people can use through the Apple Store that is related to people managing their accounts with The Rock Insurance Company. As well, we would create a Social Media presence for The Rock Insurance Company on Instagram, Pinterest, and Google+.

Technographic Profile Building

In Figure 1 shows a Technographic Profile (Social Media Models, 2016) for The Rock Insurance Company that I will explain below where the company will situate themselves:

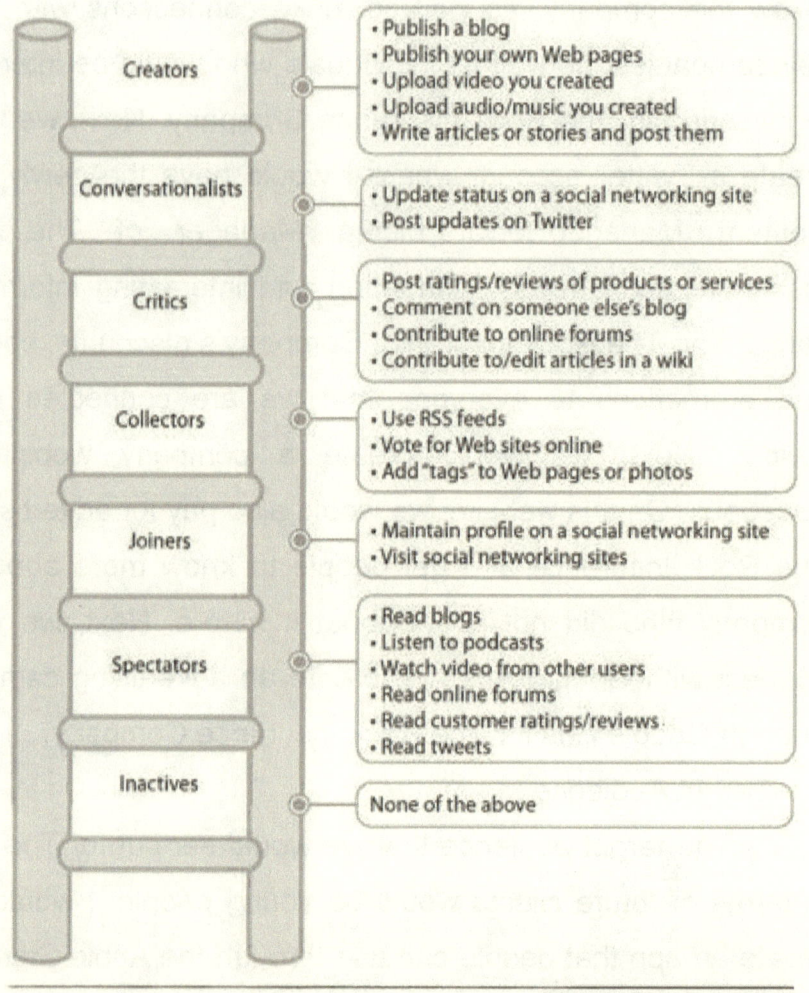

Figure 1: Technographic Profile Building

The Rock will be a moderate creator, high on conversationalists, low on critics and good with collectors, high joiner, and good spectator and not all inactive. Beneficial to the Rock Insurance Company

A Social Media Campaign will help to do three things for The Rock. It will help to increase its public profile, to gain more customers for the company and to maintain connections with new and existing customers.

Social Media is a fantastic way to improve the public profile of any organization. Social Media has become a huge player in this with many people not even turning on their television sets anymore and more people plugged into technology. The advancements of mobile devices and hardware devices in computer technology have made it possible for Social Media to anywhere at any time. The Rock needs to be a part of these tremendous advancements in technology.

Many of The Rock's potential new and existing customers are using Social Media. By The Rock participating and utilizing the influences that Social Media has over society today, The Rock will be building a stronger financial present and future for the company. As well, as mentioned previously, many of The Rock's new and existing customers are using Social Media. The company can use this technology in order to keep in touch with their customers in order to find out if new events have happened in their lives (such as on Facebook) in order to offer special promotions for insurance products.

Setting Goals

The Rock can set a one to two-year goal for the Social Media campaign. If the Rock has not improved their sales by at least 30% over this timeframe, then they can choose to opt out of this technology.

In conclusion, this section has discussed the use of The Rock Insurance Company case study using Social Media as a means to increase their business profits.

This section will also talk about the power of the media in encouraging social justice campaigns when it comes to those people who have disabilities as just one example.

Their media is designed to help students understand sexism and the toll it exacts on both men and women. They offer over 12 hours of media activities - including but not limited to - exercises designed to reveal the socially-constructed nature of gender roles, the normalcy of violence in our lives, and the institutionalized and interpersonal forms of power that perpetuate sexism. In one activity, for example, students are asked to identify rules of behavior for men and women, the ways in which they were taught those rules, the advantages and disadvantages of the rules, and the consequences for ignoring them.

Ableism

The disability rights movement has become a more organized and cohesive movement in the last 30-40 years. Ableism is one of the more complex forms of oppression to address, given the wide range of disabilities people experience, but the movement has been unified in "rejecting the notion that being disabled is an inherently negative experience or in any way descriptive of something broken or abnormal" (Adams,

Blumenfeld, Castaneda, Hackman, Peters & Zuniga, 2000). Disability advocates argue that becoming disabled is both a loss and gain, that living with a disability is simply another interesting and meaningful way to live, and that people experience oppression and discrimination not because of the disability itself, but because of other people's beliefs and prejudices.

In designing a curriculum and classroom activities to combat ableism, Griffin, Peters & Smith (2007) avoided those activities that, while well-intentioned, might perpetuate the notion that a disability is a deficiency. For example, asking students to "live" with a disability for a day inadvertently reinforces the idea that a disability is an individual deficiency, rather than focusing on disability in the larger context of oppression as an institutional, cultural, and societal phenomenon. Indeed, token efforts at addressing the topic of disability generally do manifest as so-called "disability awareness days" and tend to include such "disability simulations," which has been "long condemned by disability rights activists as promoting cultural attitudes that are ableism in nature" (Lalvani & Broderick, 2013). Instead, Griffin, Peters, and Smith (2007) ask students to identify how socialization might have influenced their beliefs about disability, educate students on different types of disabilities, and emphasize the socially-constructed nature of the disability. Students are given opportunities to interact with individuals with disabilities in a question and answer format and participate in group activities such as creating a vision for an inclusive and accessible society.

In conclusion, because social justice is such a contested issue, it's worthwhile to take a closer look at the controversy surrounding it. Even social justice scholars acknowledge that the field is marked by disagreement as much as it is by the sameness of opinion. In the end, the only course of action may be an agreement to disagree, as long as each side has the freedom to express its views. Ironically, both conservatives and liberals believe their freedom of expression is being compromised by the other, particularly in the classroom. Liberals also believe academic freedom is being compromised, but believe the conservative right is responsible.

This section will also discuss the importance of leadership styles when it comes to the goals of achieving a strong social media online personal branding presence and some of the international forces which are involved when it comes to your online audience.

"The power of money is the most dependable power" (Kant, 1983). The research questions of this thesis proposal are: how does economic interdependence affect U.S. foreign policy? How does the US-Saudi relationship challenge the democratic peace theory? The research methods to be employed in for this thesis include qualitative research methods of historical relationship along with quantitative research methods into interdependence utilizing Blanchard and Ripsman (2001). The world we live in today contains many of the attributes described by Fukuyama in 1989, however, far from ending history the proliferation of free-market economics, democratic governance, and international non-governmental entities served to highlight some troubling reminders that we have simply turned the page (Fukuyama, 1989). The persistence of oppressive non-democracies not only to survive but thrive amongst a sea of democratic reform is astonishing. In 2015, Saudi Arabia was one of twelve states Freedom House declared as "The Worst of the Worst" (Puddington, 2015) along with North Korea and Syria. While actions and rhetoric directed towards Syria and North Korea are touted as efforts to free the oppressed, the Saudi's reinforce their tyrannical apparatus with western arms and are simultaneously heralded as reformers. Saudi Arabia is uniquely able to finance extremism, suppress calls for democracy, discriminate women and minorities, forbid freedoms of speech, religion, assembly, press, as well as, practice archaic public beheadings and crucifixions, and continue to enjoy unfettered support from the proposed 'leader of the free world', the United States (US). The difference between US posturing towards Syria and Saudi Arabia are quite apparent, what explains why two states classified as the worst oppressors of freedom in the world are viewed and treated differently?

We will choose a leader from history who is admired and carefully examine their leadership style from a Social Psychology point of view. Similarly to the Barnes, Humphreys, Oyler, Pane Haden & Novicevic (2013) article that profiles Jerry

Garcia, will discuss which leadership style discussed in this unit was employed by my admired leader. As well, this essay will begin with a summary of the approaches and theories discussed in this unit. This essay will be sure to include in this essay a summary of Bass' leadership approaches, a summary of the follower-focused leadership theories: servant leadership, authentic leadership, and leader-member exchange (LMX). This essay will also discuss the concept of leadership and the importance of leadership, and explain why the selected the style chosen for the leader. This essay will discuss the appropriateness or inappropriateness of the style exhibited by the leader selected. The leader that has been selected is the 32nd President of the United States Franklin D. Roosevelt, otherwise known as FDR.

Background on FDR

Franklin D. Roosevelt created the New Coalition Deal in the United States during The Great Depression which unified labor unions, White southerners, ethnic Whites and African Americans to galvanize in support of the Democratic Party. Franklin D. Roosevelt was President of the United States from1933 until his death in 1945 and was president of America for four consecutive terms.

Analysis of Leadership Style

Barnes, Humphreys, Oyler, Pane Haden & Novicevic (2013) use Jerry Garcia to discuss the possibility of shared leadership being used for leadership styles and models, however, understand this concepts limitations when one considers the effects of world hierarchy. Franklin D. Roosevelt did not run America in the exact same fashion as Jerry Garcia who is also a notable leader, however FDR was effective in galvanizing various separated factions of American society and unifying these forces so that they could benefit from the improved changes of the Democratic Political Party, as well as to work towards getting America through The Great Depression.

FDR was also known to be a great listener which is a skill that Barnes, Humphreys, Oyler, Pane Haden & Novicevic (2013) also note as a key element in a more shared leadership style. Considering the research conducted by Barnes, Humphreys, Oyler, Pane Haden & Novicevic (2013) based on Jerry Garcia, FDR, as well as a more recent President of the United States Barack Obama just to make a brief mention of would serve as close examples to discuss and to exemplify the points that Barnes, Humphreys, Oyler, Pane Haden & Novicevic (2013) made in their research.

War and Peace

What causes war and peace? The global state of affairs today suggests we are far from understanding this pivotal question. Realists postulate that given the anarchic self-help nature of the international arena states are inclined to grab as much power as they can, hold onto it and will always put their interests above that of the group. From this viewpoint power and defence are key, essentially realists tend to fall into two camps, the defensive realists, who claim the anarchic system tends to balance itself when defensive efforts provide enough security against potential rivals; whereas, offensive realists see the system itself as the instigator of conflicts. Despite the differences in realist thought they both essentially assert that great power will seek more power in order to protect their interests regardless of the label 'offensive' or 'defensive' (Mearsheimer, 2001). Liberals, on the other hand, view the world as a conglomeration of states that have the ability to work together through international institutions, democratic ideals, and trade to bring some semblance of order to the chaos. Although realism has had an incredible hand in shaping our world and continues to dominate defence strategies it is liberal 'peace' theories that dominate political discourse and often used to push the proliferation of democratic principles the globe over. These liberal principles have led to interdependence, globalization and the international organizations we see today. The liberal concept that has been the dominant force behind efforts to explain the decline in conflict (relatively speaking) in the world is the democratic peace theory.

The modern democratic peace theory can trace its origins to Immanuel Kant's seminal work, *Perpetual Peace*, claiming it may be possible to rid the world of wars indefinitely through the spread of republicanism, interdependence and ultimately an international body encompassing all constitutional republics (Kant, 1991). Doyle used Kant's work to lay the foundation for what we consider 'liberalist peace' today, claiming liberalism consisted of the existence of three essential rights; the freedom from unnecessary authority (restricting freedoms of thought, speech and press etc.), as well as, common social rights such as equality, healthcare access, employment etc. and the third, democratic representation, would be used to ensure the continued existence of the first two sets of rights (Doyle, 1983). It is these principles that the statement 'a free and just society' is based on, where individuals have fundamental rights; the states, are provided the right to rule via these free persons and the economic side of the system relies on internal and external supply and demands principles (Doyle, 1983). Building on Doyle's work, Bruce Russett examined dyadic relationships after WWII which supported the democratic peace, laying the foundation for the normative and institutional dynamics thought to explain the democratic peace (Russett, 1993).

Democratic peace theory tends to focus on normative and institutional dynamics. The *normative* argument claims that democratic states view each other as friendly partners who share similar values, cultural affinities, and norms; therefore, they tend to choose diplomacy instead of militarized conflict to settle disputes (Maoz & Russett, 1992, 1993). The institutional argument claims that the democratic structure of states fosters collaboration, compromise and prevents militarized confrontation by producing audience costs, thereby, risking the loss of electoral support by pursuing conflict (Lake, 1992; Russett, 1993). Many empirical studies that have shown Democratic states are indeed more peaceful towards others whom they consider democratic (Maoz & Abdolali, 1989; Bueno de Mesquita & Salman, 1992; Russett, 1993; Ray, 1995; Rummel, 1996; Weart, 1997). However, most studies conclude that democracies are more (not less) aggressive towards non-democratic regimes, meaning their democratic pacification is not translated universally (Russett, 1999).

Critics of democratic peace have long attempted to explain what other factors could be responsible for peace (or lack of militarized conflict) often associated with democratic peace, questionsg its validity both theoretically and empirically. Several international relations scholars allege that similar priorities and interests ushered in the west following the Second World War rather than democratic norms and institutions (Layne, 1994; Rosato, 2003). Additionally, because of the significant correlation between economic interests, trade, and peace, recent challenges explore whether or not it is these capitalist principles instead of a democracy that inhibit dyadic conflict. Capitalist proponents claim that costs, loss of productivity, the increasing mobility of wealth, as well as, the rise of the intellectual economy, makes seeking wealth through domination more problematic and less productive. Therefore, the more developed and economically interdependent states are the less likely they are to engage in conflict (Gartzke, 2007; Gartzke & Hewitt, 2010). While democratic peace scholars assert capitalism is an epiphenomenon of democratic ideals, thus, its validity does nothing to refute democratic peace theory (Russett, 2010; Dafoe, 2011). However, dismissing capitalist peace outright does nothing to further the scholarly debate or explain the rise and prosperity in Asia and elsewhere, many of which have long enjoyed peaceful relations with western democracies. Many newer democracies in Asia had welcomed in capitalist principles far before democratic ideals, while some remain autocratic, leading some to believe it is capitalism that promotes democracy, not the inverse (Weede, 2005).

Again, if the democratic peace theory claims democracies are more aggressive towards toward non-democracies and will often choose confrontation, it fails to explain the peace, compromise, and cooperation between democratic and non-democratic states in the world. Although the United States and Saudi Arabia have every reason to oppose one another on both normative and institutional levels, they have not engaged in militarized conflict since Saudi Arabia became a state. In fact, Saudi Arabia hopes to do more business with the United States based on their KSA 2030 Project.

As an introduction to the KSA 2030 Project, the focus on the Ministry of Education is noted as the second theme of the vision:

> In the second theme, a thriving economy provides opportunities for all by building an education system aligned with market needs and creating economic opportunities for the entrepreneur, the small enterprise as well as the large corporation.

Therefore, we will develop our investment tools to unlock our promising economic sectors, diversify our economy and create job opportunities. We will also grow our economy and improve the quality of our services, by privatizing some government services, improving the business environment, attracting the finest talent and the best investments globally, and leveraging our unique strategic location in connecting three continents. (Caldera, Upeksha, Bogdanov, Afanasyeva, and Breyer, 2016, p. 13).

The KSA 2030 Project also focuses on Saudi Arabian families, encouraging them to be participatory in the education of their children, as well as to implement a strong plan for their futures of Saudi Arabian children within the family structure that can be supported and sustained (Caldera, Upeksha, Bogdanov, Afanasyeva, and Breyer, 2016). The KSA 2030 Project also aims to focus on the moral fibre of children in Saudi Arabia so that they can grow up to be strong role models for those who come after them, as well as exemplary members and exemplary citizens of Saudi society (Caldera, Upeksha, Bogdanov, Afanasyeva, and Breyer, 2016). The vision of the KSA 2030 Project is to ensure that the characters of the Saudi children are strong and they withstand with resilience all that comes their way in life by building an education system that not only focuses on their healthy livelihoods, but their moral, intellectual and professional livelihoods as well (Caldera,

Upeksha, Bogdanov, Afanasyeva, and Breyer, 2016). The goal of the KSA 2030 Project is that by 2020, 80% of Saudi Arabian families will be participating in the school activities of their children (Caldera, Upeksha, Bogdanov, Afanasyeva, and Breyer, 2016). The plan for education also includes educational events and academic partnerships.

The KSA 2030 Project also has a focus on helping to prepare young men and women for jobs of the future through education and training. This paper will focus on the children and the younger school age children of Saudi Arabia. The KSA 2030 Project also places a key importance with more trade with the United States and maintains a peaceful stance in their military actions which are promoted through their educational programming and their focus on families and children.

This article is a review of the KSA 2030 Project (Caldera, Upeksha, Bogdanov, Afanasyeva, and Breyer, 2016) of the studies related to the potential impact that the new changes of Kingdom of Saudi Arabia's vision for 2030 (Caldera, Upeksha, Bogdanov, Afanasyeva, and Breyer, 2016) with a focus on the Ministry of Education in Saudi Arabia will affect the self-assessment of Saudi students by the participation of their families. Several studies show firm evidence that the innovations of the Kingdom of Saudi Arabia's 2030 vision for education to improve the increased involvement of families in the lives of their school-age children. The perceptions of educators and students, plus their roles in self-assessment are considered along with this analysis of the techniques used by teachers and the instructional strategies implemented in the KSA 2030 Project which will lead towards world-class learning for Saudi Arabian students and spring boarded by the participation of Saudi Arabian families in their children's lives. This article concludes with a theoretical analysis and detailed examination of the nature of teacher's assessments which will lead to a foundation for a discussion of models based on theory for assessment purposes in education and superb pedagogy throughout Saudi Arabia now and in future and how the families of Saudi Arabia and their involvement in their children's schooling will lead to improved teachers' feedback for students.

The democratic peace theory has yet to explain how and why such a peace exists. Because the theory presupposes democracy as the zenith of modern governance it may act as a barrier to alternative explanations and limit the advancement of peace theories. Furthermore, should the democratic peace theory ever be undermined, the United State would be more limited its ability to utilize democracy promotion as a core foreign policy principle.

By examining internal US foreign policy decision making, I intend to consider whether democratic principles, norms, and values or economic and trade issues are considered more significant in American foreign policy decisions. Given the importance of audience costs in democracies, public support for military action against a non-democratic party than another democracy. Carrying out a survey to gauge public perceptions should be developed to determine this correlation. Adding economic and trade data within the survey could also provide insight into whether or not there is a significant difference when compared to democratic norms. Carrying out two separate surveys with one country being labeled democratic yet with little to no trade and/or economic interdependence and another non-democratic with significant trade and economic interdependence, could also serve to test the strength of democratic institutional and normative arguments against capitalist theory. Additionally, conducting a third survey with multiple regimes with gradations of democracy (using the Polity IV scale) and instituting trade and economic data could provide insight into whether or not democracy has a significant effect on support for the military conflict. This last survey would be beneficial because regime type would cease to be the central focus, perhaps providing more clarity over the question at hand. Additionally, by using Rippsman and Blanchard's Contextual Sensitivity Estimator (CSE), I intend to test how strategic sensitivity influenced the US response to the 1973 oil embargo by OPEC to the who is at odds with liberal democratic norms. By examining the possible hypothesis that (1) when American economic strategic interests and democratic ideals connect the promotion of both is preferred? (2) When American economic strategic interests and democratic ideals diverge, economic strategic interests are chosen?

In conclusion, we chose a leader from American history whom we admire. Similarly to the Barnes, Humphreys, Oyler,

Pane Haden & Novicevic (2013) article that profiles Jerry Garcia, I discussed which leadership style discussed in this unit was employed by my admired leader. I began with a summary of the approaches and theories discussed in this unit. I was sure to include in my essay a summary of Bass' leadership approaches, a summary of the follower-focused leadership theories: servant leadership, authentic leadership, and leader-member exchange (LMX). I also discussed the concept of leadership and the importance of leadership and explained why I selected the style I chose for my leader. I discussed the appropriateness or inappropriateness of the style exhibited by the leader I selected. The leader that I have selected is the thirty-second President of the United States Franklin D. Roosevelt, otherwise known as FDR. It is interesting to discuss this time period in history, way before the Internet was created. You have the opportunity to connect with key people in the world through your online personal branding.

When it comes to using social media in ways that are beneficial for your personal branding, there are many. Here are some of the stages and the steps to follow.

First, you need to find the groups online that will benefit your business interests, your public profile and your personal interests. You want to be a part of the groups that will advance you socially online. These will be groups that will either benefit you financially through the benefits of finding new clients, whether they are personal clients and/or business clients. You would also be wise to join groups that are linked to your personal interests and those things which you are passionate about.

Secondly, make sure and work on keeping your online personal brand a consistent one. As mentioned before, people really do not like change. If you undergo a radical change with your online personal branding, this will surely damage you socially as you work hard to try to establish this new image. This also includes name changes and any personal and physical style changes as well. In short, try to keep your online personal branding image consistent. However, this does not mean that your online personal branding image and reputation should not be growing. As you may move from a person with family and more assets in life, there is no problem sharing this information with your online network. It should occur as gradually online as it would in real life. The gradual change will help for it to be accepted.

Keep connecting with people, new and old, on a regular and a consistent basis. You should not have any reason to only contact the people that you are connected to online only once a year if not less. This is also where a blog comes in handy because it would be connected to your online social media network and you would always be reaching out to your online friends and network.

It is great to be a specialist in an area, however, the more that you show diversity in the kind of information that you present through your online personal branding, the more different and the more diverse people that you will draw to you in order to expand your online network and also potential clients for your business.

Get to know the key social media influencers online. Understand the way that they operate and study their techniques. There is a lot you can learn from emulating some of their practices in order to improve your own online personal branding.

The next chapter will discuss the importance of protecting your online personal brand.

Protecting your personal brand

In this chapter, we will discuss the importance of protecting your online personal brand. Some of the key things to keep in mind are ensuring that your domain name is protected and that you are keeping up with the payments on it. The fees are usually nominal and it is worth it in order to make sure no one else takes your domain name.

Ensure that you are protecting the copyright on any websites and/or material that you have online. You must do this because if it generates money, the copyright will help the money to be distributed to the right person – meaning you.

You also need to think about patients with online personal branding. If you have a unique product and/or service that requires a patent, you should really consult with a patent lawyer in your area concerning this topic.

You need to make sure that anything that you produce online is trademarked properly through your local channels. If you are in the United Kingdom, Australia, Canada or the United States or anywhere else in the world, you would need to make sure that your creations are properly trademarked by the laws and regulations of the country in which you live.

It could be a great idea to discuss with a media and/or technology lawyer about all of the issues mentioned above concerning domain names, copyrights, patents, and trademarks. There are also many online legal support venues such as LawGuru.com, Rocket Lawyer and Legal Zoom where you can receive inexpensive legal help.

You also need to keep track and supervise your online personal brand's reputation. This is important. You can do this through something such as receiving Google Alerts that are linked to your name.

If you choose to hire a social media agency to take care of your online personal branding, make sure they have the exact same vision of how you want to represent yourself online as you do. Mixing signals on these issues can lead to disastrous circumstances.

Make sure that when you are interacting with anyone online that you remain professional and do not mix business with pleasure while you are interacting with anyone online.

If you are in doubt of a move that you should make concerning online personal branding, ask someone you respect. It could be a media influencer, a friend, a colleague, a family member and/or a social media agency for a free consultation regarding your query. As with everything, beginning from your career, it would be great if you could establish a life and real online personal branding mentor who could help you to create the best online personal branding that you would want and you would desire.

The next chapter will discuss the outcome and ongoing effect of your online personal branding – your online digital footprint that you are creating.

Your Online Footprint

This section will discuss your online footprint. You may be asking yourself, what is your online footprint? Well, we discussed that at the beginning of this book. Remember when you did a Google search of your name in the introduction to this book. Anything that exists about you online is part of your existing online footprint.

The purpose of this book is simple. When you Google search your name, are you the online personal brander of what comes up? Do you "own" a stake in what is said about you online? Do you control your online personal image and your online personal reputation? If you do not, then someone else will. The sad part about someone else controlling your online reputation is that you may not like the reputation that you have.

This book has explored all of the ways in which you can improve that such as joining social media networks, creating attractive photographs of yourself, creating engaging audio to place online to reach out to those markets who cannot see and also those who love listening to audio, as well as creating wonderful video online for those markets who are not able to hear, as well as those people who enjoy watching television online. With the success of podcasts and blogs online, having these aspects as part of your online personal branding is important and if you have great written content only right now, you should consider adding audio-visual content. Many smartphones are also equipped with all the tools that you need to capture great audio and great visuals with sound and also without sound.

Some other things to keep in mind make sure that you always protect your passwords and keep them to yourself. Try to memorize them rather than to write them down and always make sure that you are using more than one email address with the second one at least as a backup in order to retrieve passwords if you get locked out of any of your social media platforms that you are connected with online.

The next chapter will discuss some questions to keep in mind in order to define your online personal brand.

Questions to help define your Personal Brand

Here are some questions to keep in mind as you self-define your own online personal brand:

- What is your purpose for online personal branding? What is your vision? What is your desired outcome?

- When it comes to values, what are your values? What do you believe in? What do you want the world to know about your values?

- What are you passionate about? What do you want the world to know about what you are passionate about?

- When you look towards the future, what are your goals for the following year? What are your goals two years from now? What are your goals five years from now? What are your goals ten years from now?

- What do you think are the strongest assets concerning your online personal brand? You should be able to write down about three or four descriptions that will help to define the attributes of your online personal brand?

- How would you define your online personality through online personal branding?

- What are your strengths?

- What motivates you?

- Are you reaching your target audience?

- Are you standing out from your competition?

If all of these questions are being positively answered through your online personal branding, then you are succeeding. If they are not, then please re-read this book and assess how you can improve. You can get feedback from other people that you respect. You can also create your own personal strengths, weaknesses, opportunities, and threats (SWOT) analysis in order to assess how your online personal branding is working out.

Bibliography

Adams, Maurianne. "Readings for diversity and social justice: An anthology on racism,

   antisemitism, sexism, heterosexism, ableism, and classism." (2000).

   Adelman, Clem, David King, and Veronica Treacher. "Assessment and teacher
   Autonomy." *Cambridge Journal of Education* 20, no. 2 (1990): 123-133.

Barnes, B., H. Humphreys, J., D. Oyler, J., S. Pane Haden, S., & M. Novicevic, M. (2013).
   Transcending the power of hierarchy to facilitate shared leadership. *Leadership & Organization Development Journal, 34*(8), 741-762.

Black, Paul, and Dylan Wiliam. "Assessment and classroom learning." *Assessment in*

   Education: principles, policy & practice 5, no. 1 (1998): 7-74..

Blanchard, Jean-Marc F., and Norrin M. Ripsman. "Rethinking sensitivity interdependence:

Assessing the trade, financial, and monetary links between states." *International Interactions* 27, no. 2 (2001): 95-128.

Bourdieu, Pierre. "The genesis of the concepts of habitus and field." *Sociocriticism* 2, no. 2 (1985): 11-24.

Boynton, Robert. *The new journalism: conversations with America's best nonfiction*

Writers on their Craft. Vintage, 2007.

Bueno de Mesquita, Bruce, and David Lalman. "War and reason." (1992): 13-17.

Caldera, Upeksha, Dmitrii Bogdanov, Svetlana Afanasyeva, and Christian Breyer. "Integration of reverse osmosis seawater desalination in the power sector, based on PV and wind energy, for the Kingdom of Saudi Arabia." In *Proceedings of the 32nd European Photovoltaic Solar Energy Conference (EU PVSEC), Munich, Germany*, pp. 20-24. 2016.

Creswell, John W., and Vicki L. Plano Clark. "Designing and conducting mixed methods research." (2007).

Dafoe, Allan. "Statistical critiques of the democratic peace: Caveat emptor." *American*

Journal of Political Science 55, no. 2 (2011): 247-262.4

David, Lake. "Powerful Pacifists: Democratic States and War." *American Political Science*

Review 86, no. 1 (1992): 24-37.

Dempster, Frank N. "Synthesis of research on reviews and tests." *Educational*

   leadership 48, no. 7 (1991): 71-76.Doyle, M. (2005). Three Pillars of the Liberal Peace. *The American Political Science Review*, 99(3), pg. 463-66.

Doyle, Michael W. "Kant, Liberal legacies, and foreign affairs." *Philosophy & Public*

   Affairs (1983): 205-235.

Frederiksen, J. R., and B. J. White. "Reflective assessment of students' research within an inquiry-based middle school science curriculum." In the *annual meeting of the American Educational Research Association, Chicago, IL*. 1997.

Fukuyama, Francis. *The end of history and the last man*. Simon and Schuster, 2006.

Gartzke, Erik. "The capitalist peace." *American journal of political science* 51, no. 1 (2007): 166-191.

   Gartzke, Erik, and J. Joseph Hewitt. "International crises and the capitalist

   peace." *International Interactions* 36, no. 2 (2010): 115-145.

   Goldenberg, Barton J. *The definitive guide to social CRM: Maximizing customer relationships with social media to gain market insights, customers, and profits.* Pearson Education, 2015.4

Griffin, Pat, Madelaine L. Peters, and Robin M. Smith. "Ableism curriculum design." *Teaching for diversity and social justice* 2 (2007): 335-358.

Kant, Immanuel. *Perpetual Peace and Other Essays: On Politics, History, and Morals.*

Hackett Publishing, 1983.

Labrecque, Lauren I., Ereni Markos, and George R. Milne. "Online personal branding:

processes, challenges, and implications." *Journal of Interactive Marketing* 25, no. 1 (2011): 37-50.

Lalvani, Priya, and Alicia A. Broderick. "Institutionalized ableism and the misguided

"Disability Awareness Day": Transformative Pedagogies for teacher education." *Equity & Excellence in Education* 46, no. 4 (2013): 468-483.Layne, C. (1994). Kant or Can't: The myth of the democratic peace. *International Security*, 19(2), 5-49.

Linton, IN. "Five Stages of Business Buying Decision Process," Chron. New York,

New York: Hearst Newspapers, 2017.

Maoz, Zeev, and Nasrin Abdolali. "Regime types and international conflict, 1816-1976." *Journal of Conflict Resolution* 33, no. 1 (1989): 3-35.

Maoz, Zeev, and Bruce Russett. "Alliance, Contiguity, wealth, and political stability: Is the lack of conflict among democracies a statistical artifact? 1." *International Interactions* 17, no. 3 (1992): 245-267.

Maoz, Zeev, and Bruce Russett. "Normative and Structural causes of democratic peace, 1946–1986." *American Political Science Review* 87, no. 3 (1993): 624-638.

Meanwell, Michael. The Wealthy Writer. New York, New York, Writer's Digest Books, 2003.

Mearsheimer, John J. *The tragedy of great power politics*. WW Norton & Company, 2001.

Mousseau, Michael. "Coming to terms with the capitalist peace." (2010): 185-192.

Oneal, John R., and Bruce Russett. "The Kantian Peace: The Pacific benefits of democracy, interdependence, and international organizations, 1885–1992." *World Politics* 52, no. 1 (1999): 1-37.

Peters, Tom. "The brand called you." *Fast company* 10, no. 10 (1997): 83-90.

Puddington, Arch. "Discarding Democracy: A Return to the Iron Fist." *Freedom in the World 2015* (2015).

Ray, J. L. (1995). Democracy and international conflict.

Rosato, Sebastian. "The flawed logic of democratic peace theory." *American Political Science Review* 97, no. 4 (2003): 585-602.

Rummel, Rudolph J. "Power Kills: Democracy as a Method of Nonviolence, New Brunswick, NJ: Transaction." *Google Scholar* (1996).

Russett, Bruce. "Capitalism or Democracy? Not so fast." (2010): 198-205

Russett, Bruce. *Grasping the democratic Peace: Principles for a post-Cold War world.* Princeton University press, 1994.

Schawbel, Dan. *Me 2.0: 4 steps to building your future.* Diversion Books, 2015.

Small, Melvin, and Joel David Singer. *Resort to Arms: International and civil wars, 1816-1980.* Sage Publications, Inc., 1982.

Social Media Models. *Social Technographics Ladder.* United States: WordPress, 2016.

Wang, Qingya, Wei Chen, and Yu Liang. "The effects of social media on college students." (2011).

Weart, Spencer R. *Never at War: Why democracies will not fight one another.* Yale University Press, 1998.

Weede, Erich. *The balance of power, globalization and the capitalist peace.* Liberal-Verlag, 2005.

Zimmerman, Barry J., and Rafael Risemberg. "Becoming a self-regulated writer: A social

cognitive perspective." *Contemporary educational psychology* 22, no. 1 (1997): 73-101.

Acknowledgements